Top Coaches Share

Their Personal

Action Strategies

11 Top Coaches share their very personal stories and strategies for overcoming challenges, creating new levels of passion and motivating themselves to create amazing success in their lives and work.

Top Coaches Share Their Personal Action Strategies

Top Coaches Share Their Personal Action Strategies

Published by
Foundation Coaching Group Inc
POBOX 26008
205 5 AVE SW
Calgary, Alberta
T2P 4L2
Canada

ISBN 978-0-9809077-2-8

Copyright © 2007 David Wood, PCC, Eng Yasmin Abouelhasan, Helene Desruisseaux, Laura Rubinstein, CHT, Martyn A. Dell, Josephine Romano CCC, CSAP, Gaye Wilson, PhD, Lisa Smith, MHT, NLP, CC, CCE, Faith Zimmerman, CCC, PCT, Kathi Frank, Lori Smith.

All Rights Reserved.

No part of this book may be used in any form, without permission of the publisher.

Dedication

This book is dedicated to our clients and the privilege of serving you.

Top Coaches Share Their Personal Action Strategies

Other Volumes

Top Coaches Share Their Extreme Self Care Strategies

Top Coaches Share Their Personal Power Strategies

Top Coaches Share Their Personal Action Strategies

Acknowledgements

Wow, this is the third book in the series, in one year! And with this book we are making the leap from digital book to printed book. Very Exciting and I am so proud to be part of Top Coaches Share project.

I want to extend my appreciation to all the authors who are participating in this book. A special thank you to Gaye Wilson for her edit of the first draft and all the other coaches that helped set us in the right direction to make such an enormous impact to our clients and the world.

I am sure that I can speak for all the coaches in this book by saying; we hope that you enjoy the stories and strategies. But most importantly we encourage you to put them into action!

Lori Smith
Foundation Coaching Group
Coach/Author/Publisher

Top Coaches Share Their Personal Action Strategies

Top Coaches Share Their Personal Action Strategies

Table of Contents

Forward by Terri Levine 11
Make a difference in your OWN life. 13
Propelling Into Action 33
Action Strategies for Success 47
What If You Feel Like A Failure? 71
Live YOUR Inspired Life 79
Move Your Life, Career and/or Business to the Next Level 95
My Top 10 Motivational Strategies 107
Inspired Actions 119
The Amazing Journey: Coming out the Coaching Way 133
Taking Action is a Pleasurable Journey 161

Top Coaches Share Their Personal Action Strategies

Top Coaches Share Their Personal Action Strategies

Forward by Terri Levine

As a coach and mentor, one of the most frequent questions I am asked is "What strategies do you personally use in your life and business?" Of course the answer is not easy to give in a normal conversation. The fact that you are reading the words on this page indicate that you are asking that same question.

Maybe you are already a personal, business, family or career coach but would like to take your business to the next level. Maybe you are toiling away at a job that doesn't energize you and would like to make that step into the world of coaching. Or maybe you are just looking for strategies to improve your own life, business or relationships. Where ever you are right now, you are searching for answers.

Lori Smith has compiled a comprehensive source of strategies to help you find the answers to your questions. She asked 11 top coaches to share their personal action strategies and presents the invaluable answers here.

These coaches are world renowned and at the top of their careers. They specialize in a variety of practices and are well trained experts in their fields. I am proud that several are graduates of my Coaching Institute. You will find their insights invaluable in the pursuit of your goals. This is your chance to "pick the brains" of today's leading coaches. Dig in and enjoy!

My Goal Is YOUR Success!
Terri Levine, The Guru of Coaching SM
President Comprehensive Coaching U, Inc.
727 Mallard Place, North Wales, PA 19454
http://www.CoachInstitute.com
(877) 401-6165

Top Coaches Share Their Personal Action Strategies

Top Coaches Share Their Personal Action Strategies

Make a difference in your OWN life.

By David Wood, PCC

It can be nerve-wracking to put your frailties out there. Most of us would rather sweep any embarrassing incidents under the rug.

My question for you is - what would you like to clean up in your past? Don't take this on as a 'have to' - just think: 'What would be a load off my shoulders if I made it right?'

Skeletons in Your Closet

You want real freedom? More than you ever imagined? Do you have skeletons in your closet? Of course you do; we all do. I define a 'skeleton' as anything you've done in the past that you feel was wrong, feel bad about, would like the world not to know, or are still hiding. Let's start with the easy ones... What do you regret, but have never apologized for? What are you still carrying guilt about? Who do you never want to bump into, because you feel uncomfortable about something? Is there something you are worried someone might find out some day? Think about it - absolutely anything about you or what you have done that you are hiding? I invite you to pause now for 5 minutes and make a list. Trust me - it will be worth it.

Now before we jump into how to free yourself, once and for all from these 'skeletons', let's go even deeper so we cover everything. Have you ever stolen something that was never publicly known? Have you had an affair that is still secret? Are you terrified people will find out you are gay? Did you ever take advantage of someone? What lie did you tell that has not been found out? Only you can know what you have been carrying around - let's add it to the list. And I promise you - no matter how small or how big, you CAN be free of it.

How Can We Be Free of Our Skeletons?

Now how can we be free of these deeds of the past? I've heard a lot of rationalization about how we should just 'let go of it', or write a letter and burn it, or some other action that bypasses dealing with the person who was involved. Oh - and check out this great line to try and justify doing nothing: 'It doesn't really bother me'. If you haven't thought about it in 3 years, then fine. If you honestly feel good about it, then fine. If not - then consider you've just gotten used to this like a heavy weight on your back. You've probably forgotten what life was like without it!

In fact - I've tried to justify most of this myself at some time in the past! This is because telling the person involved, my parents or my partner was the LAST THING I WANTED TO DO. I was, of course, hiding my skeletons for a reason: I was scared of the consequences of people finding out. If I look back at all my skeletons in the past, I was afraid of being made fun of, being yelled at, being bad mouthed in public, being embarrassed in front of a group, being ostracized by society, and even going to prison. I invite you to write down (yes, now) the consequences you could face by getting free of this skeleton or weight. It's a critical step on the way to moving through it.

The Secret

The secret is to come clean and tell the truth to the person you most fear telling. In fact - that's how you know they are the right person to tell, because that's where your fear. That's your demon to confront before you may grow and soar. Yes - this is a radical approach. Many people die with their skeletons, and with the heavy fear of being found out. However, if you come clean, if you are extraordinarily bold, if you decide that living with your head held high and the peace of true integrity is more important than anything else in life....

If you risk everything you hold dear to tell the truth, then your growth and peace will be unsurpassed.

Take a look inside. Are you stirred right now to clean something up? If so - then the best time to do it is now. If you choose to risk the consequences - if you choose personal freedom over fear of consequences, then pick up the phone and come what may.

WARNING: While the consequences are often pleasant, this can in no way be guaranteed. The whole point of this is you may face some unpleasant consequences - which is exactly WHY you've been hiding it. Some of the worst things I can imagine are: you could lose for example your partner, your family, your business, your life, or go to gaol (jail). If cleaning this up could have legal consequences, I recommend consulting a lawyer so that you know what you are dealing with. And then you can make your choice.

Top Coaches Share Their Personal Action Strategies

If you find it too big to clean up right now - if the fear has too great a hold on you - bear in mind that this can be handled a couple of ways. It can be over in 5 minutes from now - sometimes with shallow breath and sweaty hands. Or - it can be a process. It took me two years to finally clear my biggest skeleton with my close family, and the person involved. The choice is yours. To reassure you that you are not alone in this, I'm going to give you an example of a difficult skeleton I recently cleaned up in my life, how I did it, and the result I got.

Once every six months I would drive past the residential college at which I boarded when I was eighteen. And each time I would feel a tiny twinge of guilt at what I had done. While a student, I had taken the sign from the front of the college. In fact I did it twice! (Two separate signs). The signs were never returned. At the time, being drunk and with friends, it seemed like a daring adventure. In some circles I was a hero, and the college never found out. More recently, however, it felt like vandalism plain and simple - and I felt ashamed of it.

I must have mentioned it on three separate occasions to my partner, who finally said 'Why don't you clean the damn thing up and stop bugging me?' I think it took another 6 months for me to decide I was willing to risk, and accept the possible consequences of cleaning this up - embarrassment, fines, ostracism from a community, and even a police record. And in return? Integrity, truth, and knowing I was doing the right thing by another human being(s).

With racing heart I dialed the phone number of the college, and asked to speak to the current Principal whom I'd never met. (Heads up: in these calls the person is NEVER available first time. Nature's way of making you sweat it out) After introducing myself I said something like this: 'Sir, you may find this a very unusual call. I did something a long time ago that I'm not proud of, and I'm calling to clean it up. I stole a sign from the college and never gave it back. And to make matters worse - I did it twice. Can you please tell me what these things cost so I can reimburse the college?"

As you might imagine there was a period of silence. His first question was to ask when this happened. His surprise came clearly through the phone when I answered 1989! He then seemed intensely interested to know what would motivate me to make such a call after fourteen years. I explained that I had found that every time I had cleaned something up in my life, I felt better about myself. And the scarier and more uncomfortable the clean up - the more freedom I gained in my life.

He gave me a figure and we arranged a donation to the college to cover it. (And he said my timing was impeccable, as they had just lost another sign!) To my great relief, that was it.

Action: The Result

I don't promise that the results will always be what you want. But in this case:

1. I felt absolutely fantastic - an enormous high
2. The college got a new sign
3. Two weeks later I received a personal invitation from the Principal to attend an opening ceremony for a new wing of the college, and to view the new sign! (I hadn't been welcome in that college for 14 years, so I felt wonderful to be invited to such an event)
4. Would you believe the Prime Minister of Australia was speaking at the ceremony? And - with perhaps 300 people attending, my partner and I were two of the few people to be personally introduced. The press photographer happened to snap this pic: www.life-coaching-resource.com/pmpic.htm

It's weird huh? I called to clean something up, and ended up meeting the leader of my country.

Bear this in mind: life is FOR you, not against you. When you clean something up, it always works out in the long run. The more fearful you are, the greater the growth. And if you get consequences you don't like - there's your chance for even more growth. So go on. Start small if you like. Or start big and work down. Make your lists and pick up the phone!

Truth-Telling (Lies and With-Holds)

"Every with-hold you have from someone, is a brick in the wall between you."

Do you tell the truth? **What percentage of the time**? 100%? Or 90%? And when you do tell the truth, do you tell 100% of it? Or 90%?

"You look great". "I don't mind". "Yes, sex is good". "Everything's fine at home". "I'm sorry". "I didn't mean to". "Something came up".

And what about the **truths we don't say** - the "with- holds"? "I'm really upset that you canceled on me". "I don't feel respected by you". "I lie to you so you'll like me". "I'm worried if I tell you the truth you'll be angry". "It's important to me that you be on time".

You're either telling the truth, lying, or with-holding. Even most of us with the best intentions DO NOT tell 100% of the truth, 100% of the time.

Why?

We CAN'T tell the whole truth - about what we want, how we feel, what we love, what we hate. Because we need people to like us, to love us, to accept us, to want to hang around us. "If I told Jill she needs a wash, she'd be upset, or even freak out". "If I told Bill I'm not enjoying sex, we'd both be embarrassed, and he might leave me". So we get to protect, hide-out, manipulate, and control.

The Irony

If we don't tell the truth, people CAN'T love us! The only way we can really be loved - **really be accepted**, is to show who we are. To be who we are. Only THEN, once you are truly seen, is it possible for someone to accept the real you. If we instead show a "front" ("No, no - it's OK that you're late"), they can only like, love, accept the "front"! Then we feel more alone than ever, and maybe even resentful. And consider this: if you don't show who you ~really~ are, how will the beautiful souls on the planet who are looking for ~you~, find you? They'll see your "front", and move on!

In *The Truth About Relationships*, Greg Baer says: "Only when I tell the truth can I be clearly seen by others. Only then can I feel ~accepted~ by them and feel that they genuinely care about my happiness (Real Love). I create the opportunity to be loved when I tell the truth about myself."

So there it is. How do we be who we really are? How do we give people the chance to see us, to accept the "real me"? Risky, but simple: Tell the Truth.

When we Tell the Truth

I recently had the opportunity to dig deep, and reveal a very uncomfortable truth. I was developing a nice friendship with a very beautiful woman, and at a certain point, had a "flash": one reason I was drawn to beautiful women in particular, was that love/affection/acceptance from ~this~ group of human beings, felt valid and important - I let it in. However, affection from people I didn't find physically attractive, I tended to devalue. Let's get right down to it - "I could be using her to feel important!!???". While I wasn't proud of this view, and am committed to moving past it, at that moment it was part of who I am, and I risked sharing it with her.

The result? It felt incredibly freeing, creating a very safe space of honesty, and brought us even closer together. When you're willing to **dig deep, find the truth, and risk sharing it**, you:

- Create a possibility for true acceptance, and real love. - Increase yourself expression, which feels great! - Get led to who you really are, and to what you really love/hate. - Grow, and find more truth, and grow, and find more truth, and grow... - Have nothing to hide - how freeing is that!? - Attract those people ready for, and looking for, you! - Lose people who drain you (i.e. upgrade!) - Give others a gift - something ~real~ - as opposed to something false. - Create a safe space for them to tell ~their~ truth!

Action: How Do I "Up" My Level of Truth-Telling?

There ARE risks associated with this practice. Particularly for those of us who like to stick to the comfort zone, please note that ~anything~ can happen - both negative, and wonderfully positive - if you do the following:

1. Write down the names of three people you would like to feel closer to - e.g. spouse, boss, employee, friend, you!
2. Next to each name, write down at least one thing that's important to you, but you would feel uncomfortable or unsafe telling them. What have you been with-holding?
3. Tell them. Setting up the space: let them know this is NOT about them. It's not about anything they have done wrong. It's simply about you, how you feel, what works for you, and that you want to let them know where you are. (Tip: If it's something you don't need them to do anything about, let them know that!)

4. Now, give them exactly the same space! The room to share their with-holds with you. Ask them: "Is there anything you would feel uncomfortable telling me?" "Have I ever disappointed you?" (What a question!). Let them know they can say anything, and you'll simply hear it, putting all your reactions aside. (Tip: If you're not willing to put your stuff aside, don't do this! If you can't control it, leave the room).

Shock them. Thank them.

I gotta tell you - after 20 years this guy was more than surprised to get a phone call from me! But I jump ahead of myself... How much did teachers impact your life? I mean both the good ones, AND the bad ones?

I was back home with my parents for a couple of weeks, and the subject around the dining table turned to teachers. I remembered a teacher who was really nasty to me in high school; I clearly remember him telling me loudly in front of a bunch of students: "You'll amount to nothing in this school, Wood. Nothing." Thank goodness I didn't believe him, and went on to top the school in my final year. But it still had an impact. I shared with my Mum (also a teacher) over dinner how sensitive kids are to teachers' attitudes towards them.

And then I said: "You know - I was a real pain at school. I mucked around in class, rarely listened, and liked to stir teachers and students alike. But my science teacher (we'll call him Mr. Fourash to protect his privacy) handled us all really well. He always maintained his dignity, and NEVER said one unkind word to the entire class. He was nothing but supportive to us, no matter how much trouble we gave him - even when he was angry. "That really means a lot to me, even today, and I probably should have told him."

Well - the trouble with sending your Mum to the Landmark Forum is you can't say something like that and get away with it. Next thing I know she's got the phone book out and is running her finger through it..."Fourash...Fourash...I'm sure he lives...here it is." And she hands me the number and quietly goes back to her lamb chops! Now come on - I mean this is 20 years after high school; I haven't spoken a word to the man or laid eyes on him since I left town 20 years ago, and here I am holding his home phone number, with my mother avoiding eye contact and suddenly interested in the gravy jar.

"Oh what the hell" I said..."There's only one time to make a call like this, and that's now."

So I dialed the number and as luck would have it he answered straight away. I said, "Hello this is David Wood calling for Mr. Fourash", and I'll tell you, it was pretty gratifying to hear him say "David Wood? You mean THE David Wood?" God love him.

I explained that this was all spur of the moment, and I was sitting at dinner discussing him and on impulse called to tell him what a difference he made to me. I explained that I knew I was a difficult student at times, and quite a few of the teachers had felt threatened by that and tried to 'bring me down a peg' or reacted unkindly. But that I had always felt his good will towards me and the class, no matter what, and even to this day it made a difference that an authority figure treated me with kindness and respect, ESPECIALLY when I was difficult.

It was wonderful to reconnect and chat briefly with this lovely man after so many years, and to share how we were both doing, and to wish each other well. He seemed to really appreciate the call, and I can only imagine that if teaching is your life's work, it's gotta feel pretty good to hear from someone out of the blue like that and be fully acknowledged for your contribution. Plus, I felt on top of the world when I got off the phone.

Top Coaches Share Their Personal Action Strategies

Who would you write to?

Are you interested in this game? Think right now - who made a difference in your life? Who would you like to thank?

I don't expect every reader of this article to pick up the phone. But it's not so hard to call your school and find someone who would be willing to forward a letter for you if they are not willing to give out the teacher's address. And there's always the phone book, or you could place a brief acknowledgement in the local paper of your home town (what a great idea!). Guaranteed someone will pass the word.

I tracked down three teachers and got in touch with them (one from when I was 11 years old, and today I'm writing the teacher I had when I was 7!). And of course it doesn't have to be a teacher. It could be a neighbor, a relative, a police officer, a co-worker, a friend. And it can be someone you knew 10-40 years ago, or someone you see every day now ;-)

Action

1. Choose someone who made a big difference in your life.
2. Track down their phone number or mailing address or email (or a person willing to forward a note).
3. Call or write within the next 7 days.

My Nightmare. My Miracle.

This one is deep. It's personal. It's a bit more raw and uncensored than what I have written in the past, so you may experience some surprise. Some of you may not resonate with the experience, and that's OK. Take what's useful, and leave what isn't. For those of you who might wish to see me or other coaches as 'flawless' or perfect, this may be an eye-opener ;-) I've written it partly because I'm proud of this huge personal achievement, and partly because I'm always sharing with you what I discover is possible.

Some of you may resonate with this…..and see an area in yourself where you are Holding. Contracted. Afraid to go. Afraid to 'let go'. And perhaps this article will lend you inspiration and strength to open up that area ;-)

This writing is for you.

I was floating in tropical paradise, and 24 hours away from a nervous breakdown. 5 times before in my life I hadn't slept for a couple of days, and each time I'd spun out into an anxiety cycle that took weeks or months of drugs to bring back into line. I'm talking about near panic, and often just worried about how bad the panic might get! Having just finished one of these 6 month rides after India, I was even more worried about some kind of chronic lifetime cycle I'd never break out of. I looked around at the palm trees, sipped my virgin pina colada, and reflected on Kristina and me swimming in the ocean earlier that day – during a Puerto Rican rain storm! Life seemed so perfect.

Yet…I was exhausted. Tension cramped my belly, my throat was knotted, and the more tired I got, the greater the fear grew - and the less likely sleep was. When it got this bad in the past, I'd broken the cycle and saved myself with sleeping pills. But they just weren't working any more. Things were spinning out of control, and I was running out of options.

I narrowed it down to this: I was afraid of not sleeping, and at some deep level, I was afraid of sleeping. In short – I was f*****. So…. I set up a phone session with my emergency 'coach ' in the UK, Kira Kay . Picture me in the open air lobby of a Puerto Rican resort, speaking into my laptop as bikini-ed women stroll past:

"I think you're ready David, to face this fear once and for all. Take no sleeping pills, whatever happens….after 3 days you're body will probably shut down if you don't sleep. Be willing to face anything – to risk insanity, to risk death….all your fears whatever they may be. And I know you can come through the other side. But you've got to WANT it more than life."

This was one of the most horrible and terrifying things I could imagine – my lifetime Achilles heel. I had no confidence that the result would be a happy healthy David…..it could be much, much worse. And I didn't want it more than life; I like life very much!

But it seemed the entire point was to face these fears…..of nervous breakdown, insanity, and perhaps at some level….death. And again, I was running out of options as the pills just weren't working. I decided YES; wanting freedom, but not truly believing it was possible.

DAY 1

I faced some of my worst demons that same day. Simply being with the fear and exhaustion. Kristina left to spend time with her Puerto Rican family, and I wandered the resort and beach….alone. This day I discovered I CAN be exhausted, afraid, and alone. And make it through a day. I learned I can feel horrible one minute, and have a profound beautiful experience the next.

A fight with Kristina topped off the day, triggering my deep fear of feeling/being alone and abandoned. In the middle of deep pain, and feeling a gulf between Kristina and I, I called a man who had offered to help me heal if I ever got off the long term anti-anxiety medication. I figured this was a good time to call him – as I was just about to dive back on it!

What followed was profound. Dr. Jo showed us, over the phone, how I could access my deepest feelings, and release them as I shook and sobbed, or laughed. He showed us how Kristina could sit and hold my hand as I cried, giving me pure love and support. And how this extra attention from a human being (versus feeling the feelings alone) made all the difference.

Kristina and I sat on our quiet balcony and took in the bright stars that framed the palm trees and Caribbean ocean. With Joseph's voice in my ears from my wireless internet skype phone, and Kristina holding my hand, I released 30 year old emotions. I went to bed ready to face whatever came up, armed with a couple of quick tips from Joseph, and some cautious optimism. And promptly fell flat on my face.

After 3 hours in bed, and trying a bunch of techniques, I felt I couldn't take any more. I was exhausted and afraid, and Kristina was asleep. So at 1am I decided to parachute out with 10 mg of Ambien (the maximum recommended dosage). But when I pulled on the rip cord, nothing happened! In fact, half an hour later when an elephant should be comatose, my heart was beating furiously, and I could feel the panic increasing. If the max dosage won't knock me out – what will? What's at the end of the road?

I woke up feeling like crap, and scared that there was no way out. Perhaps I'm not strong enough to handle it.

DAY 2

Joseph was surprised and grateful to find out about my 'not sleeping' pattern, and the fear around it. He suggested that me feeling terrified and exhausted while ALONE, and while the feelings were keeping me awake, was NOT productive! That it would be better to either take my attention off the feelings until I had support, or…..set up support for the middle of the night!

Thank God! This was MUCH more attractive than what I saw as the full 'kamikaze-go-insane' approach. So I set up phone calls around the world in case I needed hand holding at 4am. What a group of friends I have! Friends w ho will take a call in the middle of the night, willing to listen to me shout and sob!

The result?

At 10pm that night I drifted off to sleep – pill-free! And, while Kristina was up reading! I can't remember ever drifting asleep while someone was in the room, and awake! I cannot think of anything in my life, in this universe, more valuable to me than that experience.

DAY 4

Seeing my success, and that I clearly could handle more challenges, the universe filled the resort with screaming kids – all part of three weddings scheduled for the weekend. I was HUGELY triggered by the noise, feeling very unsafe and out of control. We nearly left the resort, but I stuck it out to see what I could learn.

If you're curious about what was driving all this – what was at the core of it.....well, it doesn't really matter. And each of us is likely to have different experiences, beliefs or fears stored. Dr. Jo pointed out that understanding was the 'booby prize'. The important thing was to release the feelings. But here was one glimpse I got into what was really going on for me:

I felt how important control was/is for me, and in the middle of a 'sobbing session' I heard myself say: "If I'm not in control, things get f***** up, and people die". Wow! Talk about releasing deep stuff! I went to bed, in that 'unsafe' environment.... ...and slept.

DAY 6

The universe proceeded to the next level of challenge; the next variable ….

I had to get up at 5am for the flight back to NY. I always take a pill before a big flight (10-24 hours), or an early one, to ensure I'm well rested, and avoid feeling like crap and powerless on the plane. Well…this night I was willing to go into it. Willing to get no sleep. Willing to feel whatever came up, and to call friends and share it. I got 3 hours sleep, had perhaps the best sex of my life, and we got a free upgrade to first class. With a 30 min plane doze, I was ready to enjoy the movie, and we had a wonderful trip!

AT HOME

I had a melt-down when I got home alone: "My body is against me and is sabotaging my sleep – will this ever f***** be over!?". It FELT like I was back to square one.
But….lo and behold…..magic of great magic…..the feelings passed! And the experience reminded me that the process wasn't done, (may never fully be done) and that resisting things was not going to bring sleep faster. What a lesson! "Out of great pain, comes great insight"

THE REST

For the next four nights I slept soundly – wonderfully. I've now been pill-free for 4 months, through a variety of situations that would normally require a pill to sleep e.g. a weekend residential course, noise from a neighbor, speaking to 1000 people the next day.

What looked like being a lifetime cycle of anxiety and drugs, has opened into an entirely new possibility for me: being with myself, and my feelings....ALL of them. I now have the belief that I can face any feeling or experience. Freedom!

Action: How I broke through: 6 things

1. I don't have to face the feelings alone. (In fact, if I'm alone and they are keeping me awake, there's no point in feeling them. Put it off until I have support).
2. I can delay feeling the feelings until I have support. (This let me sleep at night, knowing things would be taken care of. I don't have to be at the mercy of these feelings)
3. I can set up support for when this experience is likely to be triggered. (For me, that's night time – particularly in an unfamiliar environment, and with noise. I had 5 people around the world willing to hold my hand on the phone while I went through the experience).
4. Releasing the emotion. (I did deep work each day on the phone with Joseph, and Kristina holding my hand. I accessed my deepest fears and sobbed my heart out. Check out co-counseling; I'm now a raving fan).
5. Being willing to go there. (Having support PLUS committing to face whatever comes up. The willingness to go dissolved the resistance, which was keeping the 'thing' in place)
6. Compassion. (I was hating that part of my body, myself, that was stopping me from sleeping. Now I talk to it; have compassion for it...for what it/I have been through in the past that is bringing it up.)

And – if you want more freedom in your life, and this article resonates with you.....perhaps you'll be moved to take a step towards confronting what's happening with you. Perhaps you'll be willing to 'go there'. If you do, I recommend support, support, support. Someone you trust.

Top Coaches Share Their Personal Action Strategies

The process Dr. Jo used with me is called co-counseling, and I'm sure there are many other support structures that may help.

About David

A former actuary and management consultant, David Wood is a certified life and business coach with a passion for internet marketing.

David has attracted over 200 well-paying clients from 13 countries - getting a huge 95% of his clientele from the internet.

He's been able to create a six-figure business doing what he loves, and now helps coaches and other professionals build their businesses, and create passive revenue streams.

His newsletter mailing list has grown to over 61,997 people in 91 countries. His web sites are listed in the top five on Google and Yahoo. He has been an on-screen coach for an Australian television series and spoken at corporations including Xerox, Ford and General Motors.

He has also been a certified snowboarding instructor, squash instructor and State 3 Player, hang glider pilot and stand-up comedian.

David offers a powerful free download called '50 Power Questions' to use for your own life, and with your clients: www.solutionbox.com/freedownload.htm

Contact Information:
David Wood, PCC
Authority on Life and Business Coaching
media@solutionbox.com
www.SolutionBox.com
www.BecomeaCoach.com
www.InternetClients.net

Top Coaches Share Their Personal Action Strategies

Propelling Into Action

By Faith Zimmerman, CCC, PCT

Learning to take action is one of the most important things you can do for yourself and when you do, your life will move forward in ways that you never imagined. You will look back on your life and say, "wow, did I really accomplish all of those exciting things?" On the other hand, taking action is also one of the most difficult things for most of us to do. Sure, there are people who thrive on accomplishing more than most people could imagine, but for the majority of us, getting ourselves to do more than our normal day-to-day feels like too much work.

Over time, I have compiled a list of the main reasons people don't succeed at accomplishing their goals. Everyone struggles with procrastination and setbacks from time to time and it by no means makes them a failure. It is human nature to run into these obstacles, but once you allow yourself to look at them closely and evaluate which ones you tend to struggle with, you can begin to work through them and change the course of your life. As you read through this list, focus on the first step in transformation, which is awareness. Look deeply at your tendencies and be aware of what is holding you back.

Reasons people fail to achieve their goals:

- They are not intentional about their goals:
    - They don't get specific enough about what they want. If you have a vague idea of what you want, you will get vague results.
    - They take life as it comes and live life by default.

- Emotions/Law of Attraction:
    - They allow their dominant thoughts to be fear related, so their fears become their reality.
    - They don't have a strong enough desire.
    - They don't keep themselves motivated long enough to achieve it.
    - Their goal is not in alignment with their values.
- Organization:
    - They don't create a solid plan of action, which causes them to feel overwhelmed and paralyzed. Since they don't schedule the actions to get the goal done, days go by and they forget about it, because life gets in the way.
    - They may not have the time, energy, belief, money, or the support they need to achieve the goal and they don't figure out a way to get those resources.
    - They don't plan for obstacles that may come up.
    - They are not flexible. They don't reevaluate and do more of what works and do less of what doesn't work.
    - Their environment doesn't support their goal.
    - Their goal is unrealistic.
    - They don't manage their time well or prioritize their tasks.

Top Coaches Share Their Personal Action Strategies

- Focus:
    - They don't set deadlines or determine how they will measure the progress of their goal.
    - They focus on their failures and negativities rather than their achievements and greatness.
    - They focus on the problem, not the solution.
- Fear:
    - They think of relapse as failure rather than getting back up when things get tough. They don't understand that relapse is part of the cycle of change and that it will most likely happen.
    - They have a fear of failure, or even of success.
    - They have negative self-talk, which leads to negative expectations and self-defeating behavior.
- Self Care:
    - They try to do too much too fast and burn themselves out.
    - They don't give themselves what they need to release stress.
    - They are too tired to do anything different in their lives because they don't get enough sleep and take care of themselves.
    - They don't ask for help when needed.

As you read the above list, what resonated with you? What is holding you back from taking action to move your life forward? Let's look at some of these in more detail so that you can really understand yourself and begin to propel yourself into action.

Squashing Fear:

It has been my experience that in many cases, when I am stuck and unable to move forward, the culprit is usually some form of fear. Fear can be disguised in many shapes and sizes: overwhelm, procrastination, stress, loss of focus, low energy – in one way or another, these can all be summed up as a form of or a symptom of fear. So, in order to kick my butt into action, my strategy is to eliminate the fear.

Many of us have come to a point of just enduring life. We allow our fears to hold us back and so we never break free and live a life of exhilaration and joy. There are two ways you can live your life: by default or on conscious intention. Most of us live our lives by default, meaning we feel that things just happen to us and so we don't decide what we want our daily experiences to be beforehand. When we live on conscious intention, however, we set an intention before we do something in order to bring forth the outcome we want. We are creators and we are here to create our experience, not to simply take what comes our way. We create everyday via the law of attraction, which states that like attracts like. Therefore everything we think, feel, say and do will attract more of that to us.

One of the most effective ways I have found to get into action is to set my intentions and work with the law of attraction consciously. The law of attraction is in effect whether we use it to our benefit or not. If you have to make a speech and you have been fearful that it will be a disaster, you are setting the unconscious intention that it will in fact be a disaster. Be mindful of your thoughts; make sure they support your goal. Instead of thinking, "oh, what if I mess up and everyone laughs at me," create a vision of how you would like the speech to go, and replay that vision over and over in your mind. That will set the positive intention that the speech will be a success. See things from the end as you would like that end to play out, and you will create that end result!

Most people try to push their fears aside, but that rarely works. The best way to combat fear is to drill into your mind the opposite of that fear becoming real. The law of attraction does not know the

Top Coaches Share Their Personal Action Strategies

difference between a real event and an imagined event. It will attract to you what you expect, real or imagined. One of the first things I do when I need to take action on something is to sit down and write out a vision of how I would like the end result to be. After I have done this, I find that I am energized and motivated, and that vision is something that I can read every day to instill that positive outcome into my mind. The more you do that, the more you will feel the fear melting away, and your confidence will rise. When you can recognize fear as a natural part of the process and decide that you aren't going to let it stop you, it loses its power over you.

You can also learn to eliminate fear and frustration from your life by recognizing the lesson in all mishaps. Don't be so quick to judge others or even yourself. When you do so, you stifle growth. This is an earth school. The reason we are on this planet is to grow and evolve as souls. We are not meant to be perfect on this planet - we are meant to grow into the souls that we are at our core. When you adopt this belief and refrain from judgment, there is no reason to fear or be frustrated because you know that there is a lesson in what you are experiencing and that lesson will bring you further in your evolution as a soul. Embrace and be appreciative of each lesson you experience, for it makes you a better person.

When you feel yourself procrastinating, ask yourself what you are afraid of; why are you avoiding taking this action? Do you want to lose the battle against fear? Or do you want to be the winner? Recognize fear for what it is: a self-defense mechanism against change. Decide to evolve past that limiting self-defense mechanism and transform instead.

Here are some activities that might help you overcome fear:

1. Define your purpose for your life. Then evaluate each action you take prior to taking it to make sure it fits in with your purpose.

2. Set your intentions for each task you do throughout the day before you take action. Determine the outcome you would like and keep that first and foremost in your mind.
3. Create a written vision each time you want or need to accomplish an action that causes you fear or anxiety. Replay that vision in your mind each time you feel fear creeping in. See yourself where you want to be, not where you currently are.
4. Keep a "Lessons Learned" log. Look over this log every few months to see how far you have come on your journey and feel proud of the person you are evolving into.

Releasing Overwhelm:

Many times, we feel stuck and unable to move forward because we are so overwhelmed that we don't even know where to begin. We can't see the forest for the trees, as they say. Being organized and creating a plan of action will help you combat overwhelm so that you can begin to take baby steps toward your goal.

If a feeling of overwhelm is what is causing the paralysis, the best thing you can do is have a dumping session. Sit down and write a list of everything you need to get done, everything that is currently floating around in your head causing you to not act on any of it. Make your list in sections: personal tasks could be one category, like sending your mother a birthday card. You might have a marketing section if you are a business owner, and so on. Put as much on the list as you can think of. The idea is to remove it from your head so that the paper can remember it all for you, thus releasing the overwhelm from within your cells. It also helps to see it all on paper in one place. What you can do after your list is complete is highlight what you plan on accomplishing today, this week, next week, etc. You can use a different color highlighter for each time frame. What you have now accomplished is you have dumped all of this clutter from your mind - you should feel lighter. You have also come up with an organized plan to accomplish each task, so you should feel less overwhelmed and able to move forward. This is the beginning of a plan of action.

A more detailed plan of action will help you to release the overwhelm even further. Have a planning session where you dig deeper into each task and break it down into baby steps. For example, if you need to have your house painted, a first step might be to research who you should request estimates from. If you know someone who recently had their house painted, you might want to ask them whom they used and if they were happy with the work. You might need to come up with a budget and requirements you would want the painter to adhere to. You might want to come up with a timeline of when you would like the work to be completed by. These are all baby steps that you might consider.

Then, follow the plan and as time goes on, reevaluate your progress and adjust the plan accordingly. You want to set some boundaries for yourself to work within, but you also want to give yourself the flexibility to make changes. Life is in constant motion and often times a plan that we set in place two weeks ago might not suit our life now. A simple way of keeping current is to always be looking for what you are doing that is working and do more of it, and what you are doing that isn't working and do less of it.

Fatigue:

Oftentimes, we procrastinate because we simply don't have the energy to be bothered. If you are feeling fatigued or are not in the mood to do what you need to do, try this: commit to doing the task for 10 minutes. Anyone can live through 10 minutes of something they don't want to do. When I do this, I often end up continuing with the task for much longer. I get involved and realize that it's not as bad as I had imagined. I have noticed that if I push through the fatigue, I often get that second wind, whereas if I sit around lethargically, I usually feel even more tired. By practicing this method, you will find that action often cures fatigue.

Reading over your vision can also help to spark you and get you motivated. Your mind and body are connected, so when you change your mind with something exciting, you will find that your body responds positively as well.

The Power of Focus:

One of the biggest mistakes I tend to make is to overload. There is so much that I want to accomplish and I try to do it all at once. I am great at multi-tasking and moving through tasks really fast, which can be an exceptional quality, but I have learned to balance it out more. It is impossible to focus on many things at once and do them really well or get the benefit you want from them. For example, I am a lifetime student, which is an area of greatness and weakness for me. I have a passion for knowledge, especially when it comes to the self-help and metaphysical aspects of life. In the past, I have tended to delve into a book and then move quickly to the next book because I can't wait to learn more information. I found, however, that I was missing the meat of the information because I wasn't allowing it to absorb into my mind before moving onto the next area of study. Sometimes it is not easy, but I make myself study one thing more deeply now before moving onto the next. I find that this allows me to not just gain the knowledge, but to own that knowledge by experiencing it and really absorbing it on a cellular level.

Focus your attention on a smaller number of things at one time and you will accomplish them with greater ease and the benefits will far outweigh trying to do many things at once. Trust me on this one!

If you are experiencing frustration in completing a task, bring your attention to this piece of advice: when we struggle with frustrations and negativities, it means that we have stepped away from our purpose – let that bring you back to your center; your place of calm and abundance. What is your overall purpose in life? What is your purpose for completing this task? Are these two purposes compatible? Are you focused on your purpose or are you focused on how frustrating the task is? Remember to keep the overall goal in your mind. While it is very important to work through a task in baby steps, it is equally important to keep the big picture in your mind so that you remember and accomplish your purpose.

When you run into an obstacle, always remember to focus on the solution, not the problem. When you are focused on the problem, all you will see is the problem. When you are focused on the solution, you will find ways to overcome the problem. Focus is always the key. Ask yourself this question often: "Where is my focus in this moment?" What you focus on becomes your reality, so be very mindful of it.

Self Care:

What if none of these suggestions are working? Well, it might be that you just need a break and that you should practice some self-care. Give yourself a time limit dependent on how overworked you are and how much of a break you deserve. If you decide that an hour is adequate, then take an hour, and do something you enjoy without regret. Doing so *without regret* is the key here. If you assess the situation and decide you need the time to recharge, then decide to give yourself that time joyfully. Then, once the hour is up, commit to getting back to work. By then, you will most likely feel recharged and ready to move forward. If you give yourself a break, but regret taking that break, you will be neutralizing the positive effects of the break, and you will just feel like you have wasted time. Be intentional and nurturing to yourself and you will be able to recharge your battery by taking a break.

Always remember to give yourself time to rest so you don't get burned out. Most of us push self-care to the bottom of the priority list. If you move it up on the priority scale, however, you will see tremendous results in your ability to act. We often treat our bodies with disrespect. We are hard on our bodies, yet expect them to perform perfectly. But our bodies need nurturing. They are the vessels that carry us through life, and if we don't take care of them, our lives will suffer because of it.

A great example of self-care that will produce almost immediate results for you is to get the proper amount of sleep each night. This is one that I have struggled with my whole life. I have always felt that sleep is a waste of time, because I'm not doing anything while I'm sleeping. I knew all the facts, that we should get 8 hours sleep a night, but I always just pooh-poohed it thinking it wouldn't make much difference. I have recently discovered that getting a good night's sleep each night is the number one thing you should do to be able to get things done. When we don't get the sleep we need, we often feel fatigued (go figure!), agitated, cloudy in our minds, anxious, and the list goes on. When we get the sleep we need, we feel refreshed, we can think clearer, we handle difficult and frustrating situations better, and we have more energy. With all of that going for us, we attract more positive things to us, rather than negative things, and when all is said and done, we accomplish even more tasks with much more ease and enjoyment. And as far as my theory of "sleep is a waste of time because you aren't doing anything while you are sleeping" goes, you most certainly are doing something very important while you are sleeping. You are allowing your body to heal, recharge and prepare for the next day. What could be more important than that? Remember to think of your mind and body as one, because they are. What you put into your mind affects your physical being and what you do for your body affects your mental being.

In summary, I hope these strategies will help you in your life journey. We truly can propel ourselves into action and it all begins with our awareness and the way we think. Choose to be aware of what is holding you back and to transforming your thought processes so that they support you in moving forward. My intention in writing this chapter was to help you move from just enduring life to being exhilarated by life! Give yourself a wakeup call and begin to activate these concepts within yourself so you can create the life you desire.

Top Coaches Share Their Personal Action Strategies

Top Coaches Share Their Personal Action Strategies

About Faith

Faith Zimmerman, CCC, PCT is a Transformation Coach and founder of Radiant Life Strategies. Her passion lies in helping people move from just enduring life to being exhilarated by life. She uses a holistic approach and assists her clients in balancing their mind, body and soul, thus bringing wholeness into everything they do. When they accomplish that, they learn to release their personal power, they create true freedom where they once felt stuck and they find themselves flowing with life in a joyful way. Her clients are then able to set and reach goals that are a true expression of their authenticity and their life purpose.

Faith specializes in assisting her clients to embrace change, so that they can transform their lives. That is the basis behind helping them to move away from just enduring life, because when we fear change, we will take what life gives us as if we have no say in the matter. Instead, Faith helps her clients to move through the fear and be the creator of their life experiences, so that their life is one of exhilaration and joy.

Faith received her certifications through The Coaching Institute as a Certified Comprehensive Coach, as well as a Personal Coach Trainer. Her vision is to affect the world through her personal coaching and through assisting others to become extraordinary coaches so that those who are coached will live more fulfilled lives.

All of her programs are custom designed to the client's specific needs and desires. She offers coaching sessions, which are generally conducted over the phone, as well as email coaching, e-courses, and workshops. For a free Holistic Balance E-course, visit her website at www.lifecoachfaith.com .

Contact Information:
Faith Zimmerman, CCC, PCT
Radiant Life Strategies
faith@lifecoachfaith.com
www.lifecoachfaith.com
 (215) 443-5076

Action Strategies for Success

By Gaye Wilson, PhD

Do you know what you want to do in your life? Do you have a To Do List a mile long? Do you make the same New Year's Resolutions year after year because you didn't keep them the first time? Are you continually working hard but never seem to get anywhere?

If you answered yes to any of those questions, you need to implement some strategies to accomplish what matters to you.

Life is short. A truism, and a cliché, but nevertheless accurate. It saddens me when someone dies young or unfulfilled. Unless we can live in an active, healthy body for five hundred years, we are unlikely to accomplish absolutely everything we ever wanted to before we die. We can, however, accomplish those dreams that are most important to us, simply by taking effective action.

When I sat down to write this article, I didn't just start writing it. I thought about what it was I wanted to say, made some notes, wrote an outline, refined it, and then wrote one section at a time. I used brainstorming, planning, chunking, shifting focus, and even some anti-procrastination techniques to complete the paper. I took effective action to complete a goal within a tight timeframe.

You can't take effective action until you know what you want to accomplish. Once you know that, you need to plan it. Each step of the way, you need to take action that will move you closer to the achievement of your goal. Only then will the action you take be effective. Any other action is ineffective action.

So what are some of the action strategies that I recommend to my coaching clients? I always start by asking this question:

What is your goal?

There is an art to successful goal setting. I recommend the SMARTER method to my clients. The SMARTER method of goal setting requires that each goal is

Specific

Measurable

Action Oriented

Realistic

Time bound

Extending

Recorded.

You'll find SMART goals talked about in business and all over the internet, but few people talk about SMARTER goals. The words for both SMART goals and SMARTER goals vary according to who you ask: these are the ones I work with.

Specific—for a goal to be achieved, you need to know exactly what it is you are going to do. "Lose weight" is not specific. How much weight? By what date?

Measurable—how will you know when you have achieved your goal? Put some sort of limit or measure on it, for example, "I will lose 10 pounds by Christmas this year". When you step on the scales on Christmas Day, will you know if you've achieved your goal? Yes, because you know your starting weight and finishing weight.

Action Oriented—action is needed to achieve a goal, any goal. Goals are not achieved by sitting on the couch watching TV. Goals are not generally achieved by one massive action, but by a series of small actions.

Realistic—this depends on a lot of factors, including the timeframe you've chosen, your physical abilities, the other things that are going on in your life. Is the goal realistic in terms of time and resources available, is it physically possible, is it achievable? Using the weight loss example again, if it's December 23rd, and you want to lose 10 pounds by December 25th, you're kidding yourself.

Time-bound—a goal without a deadline is simply a dream. How frustrating it would be to have a never-ending goal! You'd give up very quickly. But if your goal has a timeframe in which to be completed, you have a far better chance of achieving it and moving on to the next one than if it is open-ended. Time-bound also implies a timetable of planned action steps.

Extending—a worthwhile goal is one that extends you. It may extend your skills, your experience, your business, or simply your level of personal discipline. Or it may extend the amount of available floor space when you start clearing your clutter!

Recorded—a goal that is not written down is far less likely to be achieved than a written one. One of the really effective ways of achieving a goal is to write it down and post it where you will see it every day. The reminder will keep it in the forefront of your mind, and you will unconsciously work on it every day.

Read more about SMARTER goal setting and SMARTER goal achievement in my forthcoming ebooks, which will be available on my websites soon.

Planning

Knowing your goal is not enough. You have to take action. Once you know what you want to do, you need to plan it. Entire books have been written on this subject, but here are some ideas you could try.

Brainstorming

Brainstorming helps you define the scope of your project. You can do this by using a mind map or mind dump, or by discussing it with your team or support group. When you know what will be involved, start making a list of the outcomes or tasks that will need to be completed on the way to the achievement of your goal.

Mind Maps

Mind maps are a way to sort your ideas. Take a large sheet of paper, and write the name of your project in the middle. Draw a circle around the name. Think of as many aspects of the project as you can, and write them on spokes around the central theme (see sample mind

Top Coaches Share Their Personal Action Strategies

map below). This method allows you to create links between major aspects of the project, and gives you a rough idea of what you can do.

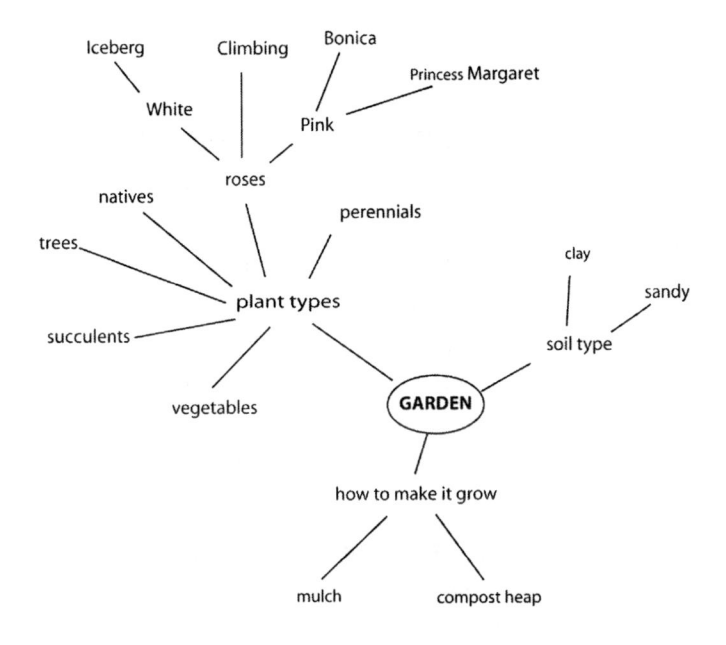

```
        Iceberg    Climbing   Bonica
                 \    |     /
                  \   |    /   Princess Margaret
                   White  |   /
                      \   Pink
                       \  |  /
                        roses
          natives         |       perennials
             \            |        /
    trees     \           |       /                clay
       \       \          |      /                  |    sandy
        \       \   plant types                     |   /
   succulents ───                               soil type
              \           |          /           /
               \      vegetables   ( GARDEN )
                          |          \
                          |           \
                    how to make it grow
                       /         \
                      /           \
                   mulch        compost heap
```

Mind Dumps

To do a mind dump, grab a large sheet of paper or a notebook and a pen (or you can do it on the computer in a word processing document if you prefer). Write down absolutely everything you have to do—everything. Pick up the kids from school. Get the dog vaccinated. Tidy the bedroom. Write the grant application. Make an appointment for annual dental check-up. Get the car tuned. Finish writing that paper. Nominate for president of the local service organization. You get the idea.

The purpose of this exercise is to dump everything that is in your mind onto paper. Don't categorize it. Don't filter it. Just dump it. This exercise can take some time. If you're still dumping a week after you first started, you probably need to hire a coach to help you get through it all!

Once you've dumped everything you can think of, you can sort your list, or categorize your list, or choose which tasks to take action on.

Create a Task List

Once you have brainstormed your project, start making lists of the phases and specific tasks needed to complete it. As you list each task, note what resources will be needed, such as personnel, information, equipment, time, finances. Project software may be useful at this stage (check out the one that is available on my website). To Do List software, such as My Tasks (available at www.kingstairs.com/mytasks/) is also very helpful.

Timetabling

Each task needs to be scheduled. Using a calendar, assign a completion date for each task, and schedule the intermediate steps in your daily planner or diary. The best way to do this is to work backwards from the preferred completion date. List the step that needs to be finished before the last step, and schedule when it will be done. Then schedule the task before that, and so on. For instance, if you were planning a birthday celebration for a special person, your backward calendar might look something like this:

Party!	October 19, 6:00pm
Get dressed, welcome guests	October 19, 5:30pm
Set the table	October 19, 5:00pm
Cook the food, wrap the gift, put up decorations	October 19, 3:00pm
Buy the food and the gift	October 17
Make shopping list	October 13–16
Get RSVPs	October 12
Send out the invitations	September 5
Make invitation list	September 1–4
Set the date	August 23

Once you have your reverse timetable, schedule each task in your diary.

Taking Action

Here is a set of techniques that I use to move me toward my goals.

Write it down

The very act of writing down your goals and action list creates an intention in you to take relevant action, and helps with the planning process (if it's written down, you won't forget it—as long as you remember where you wrote it down!). Use one notebook for everything, and cross items off as they are either completed or transferred to the appropriate project To Do List. Keep a notebook with you at all times, and one beside the bed and near the shower, to capture fleeting thoughts that will otherwise be lost. If you travel extensively, invest in a voice-activated recorder to tape your thoughts. Transcribe them every evening and rewind the tape ready for the next day.

Keep your goal in sight

List your major goals on index cards, an identical list on each card. Post the cards around your house where you will see them daily: on the bathroom mirror, next to the computer monitor, on the fridge door, on the bedside table. Read aloud the list of goals every night before you go to sleep, immediately when you wake, and whenever you see an index card. This keeps the goals at the forefront of your mind, and allows the brain to keep working on each of them subconsciously.

Plan the night before

Write out the tasks for the day the evening before. Use a diary with plenty of room—I use an A4 day per page diary—or use a daily planner such as the Dissertation Action Planner available at www.phdsuccess.com/downloads.html, which I also use when undertaking a long project. This prepares you mentally for the day, and allows your brain time while you are sleeping to get into action mode first thing in the morning. Have you noticed how much smoother getting the kids off to school works when they have set out their clothing and packed their bags the night before?

Set up a filing system for each project

Every project needs its own file or notebook. Some projects, such as building a shopping complex, writing a dissertation or setting up a complicated website, need a whole set of files. The important point is that everything connected with a project must be kept together. If you use one notebook for capturing thoughts and ideas, establish a routine whereby you transfer all the day's ideas into the appropriate project file every evening.

Work on your goals every day

Goals take time. Some goals can be achieved within a week, some take years. The only way you will achieve all your goals is to take action on them on a regular basis. If you can, do something on your goal every day, even if it is only for five minutes. The longer you spend each day on productive action, the faster the goal will be achieved.

Top Coaches Share Their Personal Action Strategies

Tell other people

Make a point of telling the people in your life that you are working on a goal. Talk about it at every opportunity (without boring them to tears). Ask for their support. A good way to keep you on track is to ask a trusted friend to call you every two or three weeks to ask how the project is going—this makes you accountable, and if you know the phone call is due and you haven't made any progress, it will be a good motivator!

Create a mastermind group

Napoleon Hill, the author of the best-selling *Think and Grow Rich* (available at www.gryphonworks.com/resources), wrote extensively about mastermind groups. These are groups of people with different or complementary skills who are willing to meet regularly to help each member achieve their goals. They can provide a sounding board, advice, resources, support and celebrations. A variation of this concept is to establish your own personal board of directors—people who are willing to help you with your goal setting and achievement, just as if you were a publicly listed company.

Categorize your tasks

Make a list of all the actions you need to take to achieve your goal. Give each one of them a time value—how long you think it will take. Divide the list into two: those tasks that will take 15 minutes or less, and those that will take longer. When you only have a short time to spend on your project, check your list of short tasks, select one and do it. When you have a longer amount of time, choose one of the longer tasks.

This list is also very helpful to get you moving when you're a bit stuck—choosing and completing one of the short tasks gives you a sense of achievement, as well as moving you toward the completion of your goal.

Schedule tasks

Every task on your To Do List needs to be scheduled, and crossed off the list when it's completed. Some time management systems recommend performing similar tasks in blocks, for instance, reading emails in one block of time, making phone calls in another block of time. That doesn't always work, so I tell my coaching clients to do their tasks the way they work best. As long as you write on your day's plan only what you commit to completing, and you actually complete everything on that day's plan, you're ahead. If you can do that consistently, you will get a better idea of how long it takes to do certain tasks, and how much time you need to schedule.

Create a routine

Routines are very helpful in creating action. Actions are partly showing up, and partly doing something. If you're a novelist, spending five minutes every week or so on your book will not get the book published any time soon. If you can set a routine where you sit down and write at a particular time every day, however, and not finish work for the day until you have written at least 2000 words, the book will be on store shelves in no time. The novelist Peter de Vries has been quoted as saying: "I write when I'm inspired, and I see to it that I'm inspired at nine o'clock every morning."

Obstacles to Action and How to Circumvent Them

You will inevitably encounter obstacles to progress, no matter what you are doing. Here are some possible obstacles to action, and how to deal with them.

- Procrastination

- Illness
- Other People
- Clutter
- Routine tasks
- Computer games
- Web surfing

Limit yourself: the Chunking Technique

Decide the deadline for your next project. Break the project down into small tasks, and then break each task into smaller chunks. Work out how many chunks you can do in an hour. For instance, if you are writing a paper and are finding it hard to actually write, limit yourself to a ridiculously low number of minutes and commit to writing something for that period of time. One of my coaching clients shifted from zero words written over a period of months to three pages a day by starting with eight minutes of writing tasks per day.

Use a timer

If you are in the mood to procrastinate by aimlessly surfing the internet, playing a computer game or watching TV, set a kitchen timer for five minutes, and allow yourself to play until it goes off. That way, you have given yourself a break, and should be ready to get back to work.

Using a timer is also an effective way to move forward with your action list. Set the timer for between 40 and 60 minutes, and work on your current task until the timer goes off. Take a short break to stretch your legs and drink a glass of water, then set the timer for another session. When you are plodding along with a task but have not set a timer, it's very easy to give up and do something else unrelated to your goals. With a timer, you can grit your teeth and persevere until the timer releases you. You will be amazed at how much you can accomplish when you use this technique.

Keep a journal

Keeping a daily journal is an extremely effective tool that can be used in many different ways. Some people use a journal as a record of their daily life. Some write a dream journal or a prayer journal. Some people use a journal to keep track of thoughts connected with specific projects. Action journals record what actions you have taken, what worked and what didn't. Spend ten minutes a day writing in your action journal, and you will find yourself progressing faster than you thought possible. Try to keep the woe is me stuff to a minimum—if you consciously avoid moaning, your brain tends to concentrate on the action and you make more progress.

Setting up a Fail Safe Environment

Successful people create environments that will inevitably lead to success. They are tailor-made to the person and the particular project. Here are some of the most common elements of a fail-safe environment.

Support system

All successful people have a support system. Your family, friends, colleagues can all help. Find an online discussion group that will help you find the resources you need, or make a regular date with a study buddy or a buddy coach. Talk to the dog, or stroke the cat when you're stressed. Walk around the block with your neighbor. Join a business network. Hire a coach.

Set up routines

Believe it or not, routines are very valuable tools for action. I know people who say they are more productive if they tackle things as they turn up, but these people tend to have multiple projects on the backburner that never get finished. If that's appealing to you, that's fine. If that is not what you want to do with your life, try setting up a routine. There's something comforting about knowing exactly what you should be doing at a particular time on a particular day, and knowing what comes next prepares the mind for the next task.

Look after your health

It is difficult to reach goals when you or your family are not healthy (I know! See my bio box at the end of this article). Whole industries are dedicated to keeping people healthy. Log onto any search engine, and you will find thousands of websites dealing with all aspects of health.

The major actions to practice are healthy eating, exercise and sufficient rest. Try to eat regularly, eat a wide variety of fresh food, and drink plenty of water. Don't skip breakfast. Keep the junk food to a minimum. Learn to cook nutritious meals.

Exercise as much as you are able. If you are relatively healthy but don't get much exercise, why don't you invest in an exercise video and exercise in front of the TV with your family?

Rest and relaxation are important to overall health and productivity. Make sure you get plenty of sleep, and take regular, short breaks throughout your day to drink water and move your body. Annual vacations should be taken to help you unwind and recharge your mental and physical batteries.

Maintaining your health is one of the best actions you can take to move you towards your goals. Without health, life is so much harder.

De-clutter

Clutter can be incredibly intrusive. It's a perfect foil to action. There must be some psychological reaction to clutter that paralyses the mind. Most people work better in a clean and tidy environment, although there are people who swear they can't work unless the place is in a shambles. Even so, clutter is an enormous drain of energy, whether you consciously notice it or not. Try to keep your workplace and home as clean and clear as possible. Get everyone (family members, subordinates, co-workers, friends) involved in cleaning up, and once it's done, put in place routines that ensure it doesn't get messy again. If necessary, hire a professional organizer to help you create strategies that work for your particular style.

Outsource

If you have too many things to do, you don't have time to fit them all in, or you don't have the skills or resources to do them, you might consider outsourcing something. You can hire somebody to do almost anything these days. If your garden is a mess but you don't have the time or energy to work on it, call your local gardening society, horticultural college or youth group, and see if they can send some students around to get credit for dealing with your weeds. Or, if you can afford it, hire a secretary to do your correspondence, a bookkeeper to do your accounts, or a housekeeper to vacuum the floors and do the washing. Outsourcing those tasks that you can't, won't or don't want to do can be incredibly liberating, and very good for the accomplishment of your goals.

Top Coaches Share Their Personal Action Strategies

Hire a coach

Professional personal and business coaches are trained to help you achieve your goals. All elite athletes have a coach; all successful business owners have a coach, a mentor or a mastermind group, or all three. Coaches provide support, structure and accountability. Hiring a coach will stretch you, develop you and cause major changes in your life.

Multiple projects with similar or tight deadlines

Most time management schemes recommend that you do one thing at a time. Multitasking, they say, doesn't work. So what happens when you have to do several tasks or projects, and they are all due around the same time? Many people suddenly realize that they have procrastinated so long over a particular project with a long lead time that the deadline has suddenly crept up, and now coincides with the deadline for another project. **Don't panic.** There is a way to get everything done.

Use the principle of chunking to divide your day

List the smallest possible task chunks for each project. Assign each chunk a specific amount of time or a specific number of repetitions that it will be worked on today. Once you've completed one chunk of time or one set of repetitions, move on to the next project, and do a chunk of that.

Here's an example. I once had to finish making 600 toy bags for a local library, plan a camp, design a website, do a proofreading job and do some photocopying. All in the same week. On the Wednesday, I sewed ten toy bags, then made the required number of copies of five pages, planned the camp menu, spent 40 minutes listing the files required for the website, sewed ten more bags, copied five more pages, made out the camp shopping list, did one hour of proofreading, took a short walk to clear my head, sewed ten more bags, created the website template, etc. Every time I got bored with sewing seams or photocopying pages, I persevered until the nominated number was completed, then moved on to the next project.

I have found that using this technique creates a super-productive day, on all projects. I think this is partly because changing focus every so often during the day gives you a bit of a break so that you are fresh when you come back to it, and partly because you are completing small, but important, tasks that contribute to the end goal.

Try it. My clients love to use this technique! Be aware, however, that this is quite tiring and I don't recommend that you use it every day.

Halve your day

Another alternative, if you only have two major projects with similar deadlines, is to halve your day. Choose one project to work on in the morning, and the other in the afternoon. That way, both projects get dedicated attention and action, and both make progress every day.

One day per week

A less effective method of tackling multiple projects is to assign each project to one day per week, and schedule some time for it on its assigned day. I know an author who only has time to write her book on Saturday afternoons, but she does it for four hours faithfully every week, and her family knows her schedule and helps her keep to it. This method lacks the momentum that often keeps projects afloat, but may be the only way you can spend time on yourself and your goals. At least if you can stick to it, you will make some progress.

Top Coaches Share Their Personal Action Strategies

What happens when you're blocked?

Shift your focus

Sometimes it happens that a project is blocked: you're missing some information or materials, waiting for action from someone else, or there's so much to do you don't know where to start. Try unblocking it by working on another project, or a different phase of the current one.

For instance, if you are writing a book and the chapter you are working on just isn't going anywhere, try writing a different chapter, or a short article, poem or short story. Write a letter, or a postcard. Do some related research. You will still be making progress, while allowing your mind some time to regroup.

What to do when all else fails

A lot of my coaching clients come to me because they are stuck. For whatever reason, they are not taking action that will lead them to the completion of their goals. When all else fails, I ask them to try one of the following techniques.

The reward technique

This involves choosing a pleasurable reward when a task has been accomplished. This could be reading that best-seller that's been on your shelf for a while, going out to dinner with friends, buying a coveted piece of jewelry, going fishing—whatever takes your fancy. But you only get the reward when you accomplish your task.

The punishment technique

The punishment technique involves your choice of action that you really, really don't want to do: donate $500 to the political party you hate, give away your best dinner jacket to charity, clean the toilets—anything that you would do anything to avoid. Like the reward technique, you only get the punishment if you don't complete your task.

Which technique you choose depends on how you work best. Some people work well with a reward ahead of them; some people accomplish more with a punishment hanging over their heads. The trick is to choose the method that will work for you at the time, and make sure you go through with it if you don't reach your target.

Take any action

Sometimes nothing is going right, and you stall completely, not knowing what to do or where to go. This is very frustrating, and more common than you might think. When you are completely stuck, the best thing to do is to take action—any action. Pick up the item on the floor closest to your foot and put it away. Take the dog for a walk. Ring a friend and ask for help. Make a list and do the first item. Wash the car. Vacuum the carpet. The very act of doing a trivial task is sometimes the impetus needed to take action on that pressing project.

Remember I said earlier in this article that effective actions are those that move you toward your goal? This type of action—the "any action" action—does not need to be directly related to your goal. Its function is to get you moving. It is, therefore, by definition, an effective action. I had a coaching client once who refused to believe it was that simple, but it is. Sometimes taking an action, any action, will get you back on track.

Evaluating

Why evaluation is important

When you've completed a project, make time to evaluate how it went. It's important to do this for many reasons, including:

- so that you can learn from what didn't work and what did;
- so that you can reproduce the actions if necessary;
- so that you can help others to achieve a similar goal (that's one reason I became a PhD Coach); and
- so you can learn more about yourself and how you work.

Knowing your own strengths and weaknesses will help you plan and carry out your next goals. Using the SWOT analysis beloved of business can help here. SWOT stands for:

Strengths
Weaknesses
Opportunities
Threats

When evaluating your completed project, ask yourself these questions:

Strengths—what were the strengths of the project? What was I good at? What went well?

Weaknesses—what were the weaknesses of the project? What was I not so good at? What didn't go well, and how could it be improved next time? What are my own personal weaknesses and how can I either strengthen them or work around them next time?

Opportunities—what opportunities have opened up as a result of this project? Are there spin-off projects or applications that could be developed? Do I now occupy a stronger position in my market that can be developed? Where does this lead? What can I do next?

Threats—are there any potential detrimental consequences of the project completion? Have I closed doors that were previously open? Am I now perceived as a threat by my competitors as a result of my success? Am I at a dead end?

Evaluation methods

Evaluation of a project can take the form of:

- images of the finished product, before and after photos;
- a checklist or questionnaire that has been tailored to the project or your goals;
- formal or informal discussion and feedback from team members or support people;
- a written report;
- a blog;
- a list of what didn't work and what did work;
- whatever works to help you revisit the project, the process and the outcome.

The evaluation needs to be in a tangible form. If you just think about how it went, but don't write it down or put your conclusions into some permanent format, you will lose all the benefits of doing the evaluation. And the benefits can be huge down the track.

What to do with the evaluation

There's little point to evaluating without taking some further action. Here are some ideas of what you can do with the evaluation:

- send the report to your boss/friends/family;
- post it on a website or blog;
- use it to remember what to do or avoid the next time you tackle a similar project;
- use it to choose your next goal.

Top Coaches Share Their Personal Action Strategies

When to do the evaluation

The initial evaluation needs to be done immediately after completion of the project or goal. It's a good idea also to evaluate its impact a month, six months, a year or five years later, depending on the goal. Some people write a formal annual report on themselves, as if they were a publicly listed company, which covers goals completed, goals not yet completed, financial statement, SWOT analysis, courses attended, qualifications gained, wins, losses, plans for the next year. These people are achievers. If you want to join them, maybe an annual report on You Inc. would help.

Final Words

This article has skimmed the surface of the many action strategies available to help you achieve your goals. Remember the process:

- Know what you want by creating SMARTER goals
- Plan your project
- Take action
- Evaluate your efforts
- Create your next goal.

Half the battle is showing up. The other half is using whatever techniques will work to move you towards your goal. The techniques I've talked about here can be used for any goal, whether it be losing weight, writing a dissertation, saving money to buy a car, starting a business or learning a musical instrument. No matter what it is you want to accomplish, these techniques can get you there.

Probably the most important factor of success is determination. If you have sufficient determination and motivation to accomplish something, you will find a way to do it. Use the techniques described here to achieve your goals quicker and easier.

Top Coaches Share Their Personal Action Strategies

About Gaye

Gaye Wilson PhD is the owner of Gryphonworks, an Australian editing and coaching business with clients worldwide. The business specializes in academic editing and coaching, and in website and ebook editing, proofreading, layout and design.

She has been (and still is, in some cases) a student, soldier, forms designer, animal shelter worker, trainer, manager, library worker, website administrator, website designer, first aid instructor, youth leader, organization and methods consultant, human resources development consultant, author, Egyptologist, archaeologist, research assistant, coach, editor, indexer, proofreader and desktop publisher. She has a great many interests, and usually has many projects on the go at once. One of her greatest recent accomplishments was completing a PhD while coping with severe Chronic Fatigue Syndrome. Having little energy to spare, and lots of things to do, she has become an expert at creating strategies for effective action, and uses those strategies to support her coaching clients to achieve their goals.

Contact Information:
Gaye Wilson PhD
GayeWilson@gmail.com
www.PhDSuccess.com
www.gryphonworks.com

Top Coaches Share Their Personal Action Strategies

What If You Feel Like A Failure?

By Helene Desruisseaux ("Derusso")

To get into action and stop procrastinating you must: set measurable goals, break them into smaller segments, set activity targets, create an accountability structure, decide on rewards and penalties.

Yeah, yeah, I know, I know, I know! How come I still don't do anything? Or I pretend to be doing something and am really "busy", but not getting any results.

I've experienced that frustration more than once in my life, and it's no fun. It feels like there is no way out. It's like being in a spider web where the more I struggle, the harder it is to free myself. The more I tell myself that I should be doing something and don't accomplish much, the more I descend into the hell of failure.

What's going on?

The more we feel like "losers", the less clear and decisive we become. No wonder most of us are so afraid of failing; it can be so hard to get back to form afterwards. And the standard advice on how to get into action doesn't work because we are either afraid of failure or feel like one already.

We're like deer frozen in the headlights, too afraid to move. The motivational books or talks give us hope for a short while, but not really, if we're honest with ourselves. How can we take risks to achieve our dreams when we feel so defective?

We might tell ourselves to change our thoughts and beliefs, but most of us can't completely shake the shock (if we are usually successful) or discouragement (if we've been struggling for a while) and the ensuing fear that follows.

What's the solution?

To make it easier to break free, we have to first weaken the ties between our thought-beliefs and our negative emotions. And it's not always possible to change our thoughts by using our thinking process. We have to work from another level.

Let's use one of my "failure phases" as an example.

I was not a popular kid always feeling a little different, the perpetual outsider. As an adult, I dreaded unstructured social events, knowing I would be boring and bored. Yet I was gregarious and lively at work so I had the necessary "equipment" to be a people person.

I could rhyme off what I should do to improve my social life…but I couldn't do it, because I couldn't rid my mind and emotions of the label acquired years before, that of social misfit. Somewhere in my psyche, I was a social failure, doomed to be well-adjusted at work and shy elsewhere.

If I knew then what I know now, I would have avoided years of pain. Here's what I would have done.

Acting has its place

We've often heard the advice: "act as if" you already are what you are hoping to be. Good advice, except it can be hard to do when you are in the very situations you find difficult (like at a party).

The solution is to first "feel as if" before you can act. When I was feeling safe at home, I should have taken some time to imagine myself more as an extrovert. Mentally put myself in the shoes of a socially comfortable person. Imagine how they must feel and immerse myself in the confidence and pleasure they would find in social interactions.

Rather than visualize myself as confident or do affirmations stating it, I have to first imagine what another person would feel like when they are confident because it's too much of a stretch to think I could feel that way myself. And let me warn you, when it's that much of a stretch, your mind will resist the exercise, labeling it as impossible.

In my example, my lifelong struggle with social events like parties made it difficult for me to really believe that I could ever change. You would think that having a prior history of success would make it easier to recover from a recent failure, and it does…a little. But hating how failure feels might trigger enough fear to make us lose our resourcefulness.

If we have a hard time believing in ourselves, it's very useful to pretend we are someone else and to become an actor. Then our fear and protective mechanisms don't kick in; after all, we are just playing a role.

So we need to act, pretend to be the kind of person that we want to be, and do it often and repeatedly. Then we immerse ourselves often enough in the desired state (socially confident, in my case) to allow our subconscious to become comfortable with it and eventually, familiar. What feels familiar feels natural, and that's the wedge through the door that we need to make progress toward our goal.

Since I had never felt comfortable and confident at parties, I couldn't make myself act as if I was. But in the privacy of my own home, I could imagine what a popular person might feel like; what she would think; how she would act. I could feel the pleasure in it all. The more I played the part, the more I felt it was familiar (to state the obvious), and I liked it. This made it a lot easier to access that confident state as me, not as one of my "characters".

That for me has been the true magic of "acting as if".

Movement therapy

Another way of getting out of "failure zone" is to change our fearful, frozen state to a more resourceful one by working with our body. Here's how it would work in my case.

First, I would observe how I hold my body, how I move and react when I am self conscious and socially shy, really noticing details. Then I would consciously hold my body in that way.

Then, I would get back to acting and step into the role of the confident extrovert. How would that character hold her body, how would she move and react; again, noticing details, then imitating the confident body language. Stand the way they stand, hold my head and shoulders the way they do, walk around, etc.

As I recall how good it feels to be comfortable in one's skin I would play up that happiness, and when I am really "into it", I would anchor it by making a gesture (such as thumbs up) that my mind will from now on associate with the good feeling.

I would go back and forth between the failure and the resourceful states, changing my body language back and forth, making sure my whole being notices the differences and is well practiced at changing states at will.

This technique by-passes our thinking and uses our bodies to entrain our feelings. It avoids the trap our thoughts can set when they second guess us into staying frozen into our tracks.

Drop the charge

We're bound to have strong emotions about our failure(s), even if we appear to have moved on. I'm a strong believer in using EFT (www.emofree.com) or the Sedona Method (www.sedona.com) to defuse the charge around past events.

Engage the mind

Now that we have done enough work to access a resourceful rather than destructive state, we can learn from our failures. After all, if one believes that life happens to teach us lessons, let's learn them so we don't have to repeat them.

Ask yourself questions such as:

- What gifts did my failure(s) bring me
- What can I learn from them

A word of warning on that last one: watch that you don't go into self recrimination, because that isn't the point. It's not about "I should have known", or "how could I be so stupid". It's easy to go there when we are still stinging from the pain and fear of failure, which is why I recommend waiting to do this work until you are more detached, or at least steady, on the whole saga.

Here is one trick to stay constructive. Imagine you are observing your life as a movie, and someone tells you that despite appearances, this person's life is right on target. Describe what might be the purpose of the failure(s) in the whole context of that life's history.

Another warning: If you answer to that was humiliation or penance, you're on the wrong thinking track.

This is no time to go solo

Which brings me to a very important point: many people find that working with the right person (a knowledgeable friend or a coach) makes a huge difference in their progress. For example, they could point out when you are stuck in blame or regret when doing the last exercise.

Taking action is really hard when you feel like a failure. In my example, I was starting from scratch without a base to build on, so it was bound to be difficult. But even if we had a strong record of success until we blow "it" (whatever "it" is), we can find it very difficult to get back in gear. We might be able to take action but make choices that backfire. We're still acting from a non-resourceful state.

It's natural to retreat when we think we failed, but feeling like a failure takes so much of our energy and emotion that it's nuts to try to get over it by ourselves. Why waste that time and extend our pain? Now more than ever, we need support. Besides, without someone holding us to a certain structure, we might not do what we need to do to recover.

Like I said, I wish I'd learned a long time ago what I know now.

About Helene

As the founder of Success Worth Living, I help people who aren't enjoying success like they should, either because:

- They aren't confident enough to take action effectively
- They don't know what actions to take
- They are stressed and overwhelmed by the demands put on them by themselves and others
- They take refuge in emotional eating or other unproductive habits
- All of the above ☺

Before becoming an accredited, certified personal coach, I spent over 20 years in corporate management, corporate training and higher education, and as an entrepreneur. So you can imagine I have seen many variations of how people deal with and strive for success.

I saw that we all waste years of our lives in stress, thinking that nothing can be done but grin and bear it.

I saw star performers retire with very few people in their lives because they were too busy to make room for them or didn't know how to be high achievers and still have real interactions with others.

I saw great people wilt away as wall flowers because they didn't have the social skills or confidence to blossom at work and elsewhere.

I saw business owners feel isolated, thinking they had to figure it all out themselves, because they had no one to talk to that was able to understand all aspects of their lives: business and personal.

Becoming more and more interested in how humans function and how we can all have better lives, I studied many aspects of performance psychology and human energy systems.

Now I can use both sides of my experience and training (business and energy psychology) to help people achieve more successful and enjoyable lives.

Come and visit me at www.successworthliving.com; I welcome all questions, comments and insights. Author of the upcoming book: "The Successful Introvert: Doing it on your own terms"

Contact Information:
Helene Desruisseaux, MBA, DNM, CPC, ACC
info@successworthliving.com
www.successworthliving.com
(519) 238-2245

Top Coaches Share Their Personal Action Strategies

Live YOUR Inspired Life

By Kathi Frank

When I am inspired, I get excited because I can't wait to see what I'll come up with next.   Dolly Parton

In today's world most people are looking for ways to have just a little more rest and a little less action. I suspect that anyone reading this book is keeping pretty busy. In fact, in a New York Times article, Timothy Egan reports that Americans are taking less time off each year.

A few statistics:

- According to the Conference Board that does research on such matters, 40 percent of employees are not even considering a vacation during the next six months.
- The Bureau of Labor Statistics finds that one fourth of working Americans don't get any paid vacation. Of those who do, only one third of them plan to take off a full week from their work this year.

Top Coaches Share Their Personal Action Strategies

Your body, mind and soul need time away from work to reinvent and rejuvenate. So why am I telling you this in a book dedicated to give "Personal ACTION Strategies"? It is because I am convinced that your non-stop lifestyle hinders you from feeling motivated to action. It is only when you can become inspired by your life that action becomes easy. So, I would like to talk about living YOUR inspired life.

First, I have a few questions for you. Is that busyness worthy of your time? Is that busyness actually distracting you from taking action in an area where you are coming from your core competency? Do you lack inspiration and therefore doubt that you will accomplish the goals that are most meaningful to your life? What is it costing you - in your relationships, in your income, in your soul's satisfaction - to be too busy to take action on those things that inspire you? What are you afraid of? What will it take to get you to live YOUR inspired life?

Ask most people about their core competencies and they will modestly confess in having nothing special. I say that a position like that is rubbish. Each and every person on this planet possesses something unique and valuable to the world. If you do not discover and develop that unique gift, the world is missing something incredibly important that only you can offer to us.

If you have ever felt that you are out of step with the rest of the world - Congratulations!!! It is the people who feel most alienated by the general population that have the most to give to all of the rest of us. That may sound like a preposterous statement, so allow me to give you one example. I could give you dozens, but will spare you the reading.

Sylvester Stallone has been a famous movie star since his original hit in 1977. Most would think that he was discovered by a successful movie director, or casting professional. At least he had connections with a script writer or producer, right? The truth is that he wrote the script, raised the money, played the lead character, produced and directed the entire film himself. Why did he do all this? Because no one else would and he knew that his inspiration came from the deepness of his being. He knew that his story, both the one on the screen and the one he has lived, would be an inspiration for others. We all *want* to be inspired. Also, we all *need* to be an inspiration.

Let's take a look at Stallone's history. He was injured at birth, which caused him to have a droopy lip and slurred speech throughout his life. He had a very troubled childhood and went stumbling from job to job for several years. When he stumbled into acting while coaching women's athletics at the American College of Switzerland, no one had any idea that he could become a superstar.

In *Rocky* he played an awkward misfit in a leather jacket, not exactly the image Hollywood was buying at the time. No one could have convinced them that the stumbling guy with a speech impediment would soon be the city's most famous actor. Yet, if he had not discovered his hidden genius of inspiration, there would be no *Rocky* series, no *Rambo* series, no Hollywood legend by the name of Sylvester Stallone.

It becomes abundantly clear that the world benefits when an individual discovers their hidden genius. If you believe that principle, you can see that you owe it to society to discover your own. Make a serious effort to find that part of you that can become inspired - then take all the chances necessary to exploit that talent for the benefit of everyone around you.

Obviously, the rewards are limitless - in dollars to be earned and also in the quest for leading a fulfilling, meaningful, inspired life. Isn't your pursuit of that calling worthwhile?

If you are struggling to see where your genius lies, try making a list of the things that come easy for you. Look particularly at the things that you do with ease that others find difficult. Whether you are willing to consider yourself a genius in those areas or not, history proves that it is in those areas that you find the most inspiration. The fact that it seems effortless to you is God's clue that you've found your area of hidden genius.

I used to get hung up on the fact that I have some trouble comprehending technology. I worked hard to overcome my lack of effective communication between my brain and electronic devices. A friend and exceptional coach, Joeann Fossland, offered me this advice: "Kathi, life is too short to perfect your weaknesses. Build on your strengths." It has been some of the most profound advice I have ever received.

It is within your unique "soul-print" that you will find true inspiration. From there, you only have to possess a relentless pursuit of those inspired goals to have a good life. That is what I hope for each and every one of you. Most people live their lives in survival mode. "Stuff happens and then you die" is the motto of the masses. What I want is for you to decide what kind of life you want and go for it. When others look at your grave marker that indicates the day you were born and the day you passed over to the spirit world, I want them to know that you dashed, with passion– not strolled, aimlessly.

Famous author, Robert Ringer, wrote a book by the title, *ACTION! Nothing Happens Until Something Moves.* The title of his book is actually a quote from Albert Einstein. His concepts are right on target when it comes to the importance of taking action. What I would like to share with you is a detailed plan for taking action that is directed specifically to your inspired life.

In order to make my suggestions easy to remember, I have arranged the segments using the letters in the word "ACTION". Follow along with me and see if any of my ideas can spark inspiration and action.

ASSESS

> *Trust only movement. Life happens at the level of events, not of words. Trust movement.* Alfred Adler

Create a system for capturing every idea that crosses your mind. Some of those preliminary ideas will be pure gold, some will be silly, some will not be feasible, some have been done by others and some will be downright embarrassing. But these are your seeds of inspiration. From these seeds you will gather up your greatest ideas. Set aside a regular time once a week to go over your list of ideas and assess which ones deserve to be taken to the next level.

Too many people let great, profitable, inspired ideas run through their minds like water running between their fingers. Have you ever had a good idea and not acted upon it only to see someone else making a mint because they did take action on the same idea? I believe that God, source energy, universal power, whatever term you would like to use, inspires each and every one of us. However, we are so busy being busy we do not hear that still, small voice that tells us how to get out of the rat race of busyness.

Determine when and where you get your best ideas and make sure you have a way to record them as soon as they come to you. Many people keep a journal by their bed because their best ideas come when they are sleeping. If you get out of bed, go to the bathroom, brush your teeth, eat breakfast, then stop to record your good idea – chances are you will not even remember what you had intended to record. Keep the pen and paper on your nightstand and record the ideas before you even get out of bed.

One of the most dynamic coaches I have ever known, Brian Buffini, confesses to keep a journal just outside his shower. He cites scientific evidence to support the fact that hot water pounding on your body causes neural pathways to open and allow new ideas to come rushing in. It doesn't work for me, but I wouldn't begin to tell this highly successful and wealthy man that his theories are wrong.

Personally, I get my best ideas while driving down the road. If I turn off the radio and cell phone, the monotony of the road noise seems to clear a space in my mind that allows great ideas to develop. I sometimes write poetry and most of those poems were loosely constructed while driving down the road. When I was able to get to the computer to record them, it almost seemed that the writing was simply a download. The thought processing was all done while driving in the silence. Rest assured, I do not try to write these ideas in detail while in traffic. Instead, I carry a spiral notebook with me wherever I go. If I have a great idea, I am able to hold it in mind long enough until I can safely write one word to describe the concept and remember to expand on the idea when I get in a comfortable place to assess the value.

You never know when an idea passing through your mind is pure genius. Take the story of Velcro for example. In 1948, the inventor of this modern marvel was walking his dog. When he returned home he noticed that his socks and his dog were covered with pesky burrs. He was curious about how they stuck to his clothing and proceeded to look at them under a microscope. He found that the burrs had tiny hooks that allowed them to hang onto the fabric. In 1955, he patented Velcro, now a billion-dollar industry. How many people, over the centuries, experienced getting burrs on their clothing and never asked why?

Write down *every* idea that comes to your mind, a few of them will be pure genius. Once the ideas are recorded, it is relatively easy to assess whether they are in alignment with your core competencies. Described by Russell Cornwell more than one hundred years ago as the "Acres of Diamonds", the bounty of ideas is available to you. If you do not have a system for recording and assessing ideas as they come to you, inspiration may continue to be on "Someday Isle".

CREATION

Outstanding people have one thing in common: an absolute sense of mission. Zig Ziglar

Once you have selected one of the ideas to develop, visualize it being fully realized. Create the scenario in as complete a manner as you can imagine. At this point, do not worry about the details. Your goal is Stephen R. Covey's principle of "begin with the end in mind." Create a clear image of what this idea will be when it is fully developed.

For demonstration, let me give you a potential scenario. You want to start your own business online. You have thought of a clever product that is perfectly suited to your core competency and it is appropriate for being marketed on the net. Take time to clarify how the product will be delivered. Will you use a fulfillment service to deliver orders? Will this product lead to a number of other products and services that will expand your prosperity? Will you be doing any travel to promote the product? Are there any affiliated businesses that you can tap for joint ventures in marketing the product? What will you spend the majority of your time doing when the idea becomes fully developed? How does it feel to be spending your time and effort performing those tasks? Do you feel inspired by that way of life?

Important to remember when you are creating your vision - it is YOUR VISION.

Do not let any experts around you tell you that your ideas are not worthy. Let's look at some biographical information about someone you may recognize Sam Walton.

Top Coaches Share Their Personal Action Strategies

When he was the owner of a small retail chain of about 30 stores, he went to New York to see if he could learn something from the big-city discounters. An executive of one of the country's major discount chains agreed to spend some time reviewing Sam's plans. Walton pulled out a few crumpled papers from his breast pocket and showed his ideas to Mr. Big. The papers contained handwritten sales and profit figures from the thriving, but small-town chain with a countrified name: Wal-Mart.

When Mr. Big reviewed the numbers, he gave the papers back to Walton and urged him to not share those figures with any other New York discounters. Instead, he was advised to go back to Arkansas immediately and to keep doing whatever he was doing to produce such fantastic results. The executive assured Walton that no one in New York came even close to the profitability that Wal-Mart was achieving as a small regional chain of stores.

Can you imagine if he had received advice from those "experts" about how to run his business when he was getting started? Many of those major discounters went broke during the next decade or two. Sam Walton's independent, dare I say inspired, ideas caused him to become the largest retailer in the world. He was clear in the beginning about how he wanted to feel in creating this retail operation. He thought about how his employees would serve the customer and how management would serve the employees. He knew how he would work with suppliers. He visualized how his concepts would result in the store remaining profitable while giving the customer the most value for their spending dollar. He only had to act on the vision he had created and the universe worked in concert with him to make that vision a reality.

TIMELINE

You read a book from beginning to end. You run a business the opposite way. You start with the end, and then you do everything you must to reach it. Gregory Nunn

Break the concept into bite sized pieces and put them on a calendar. Although this aspect of your action plan cannot be precise at this point, it is critical that you take the time to estimate how much time each step of the process of growing your idea will take. Do the best that you can and be aware that it might take even more time than you estimated.

If you are like me, when I sit down to plan the time it will take to develop an idea to its fullest it is usually a little shocking. There are so many more steps that need to be taken than you would ever think in the first place. So, be ready for a "reality check" as you go through this process.

The timeline process:

- Begin with a list in no particular order of things that will ultimately need to be done to launch your idea.
- Look at each item on your list and see what sub-categories should be included.
- Sort them in chronological order. I usually use 3x5 cards for this stage because it is so easy to move them from one place to the other. There is something about holding the items in my hand that helps me to think through the order. I'm sure it could be done more efficiently on the computer, but I can get hung up in the technology.
- Assign segments of time that it will take you to perform those tasks or delegate them to others. If you are doing this in addition to another job, carefully consider how much time you can devote to the entire process.

- Assign an estimated cost to those things that you can delegate to others. This will become the beginning of your budget later.
- When you have a specific time assigned to each task, placing them on a calendar will help you to visualize the total time it will take you to complete the process.

Applaud yourself, you have completed the hardest part of the process. If, at the end of the creation stage you feel really good about the end result. If, once you have established a timeline you feel it is still feasible. You are on the road to your ultimate inspired life.

INTENTION

> *Always bear in mind that your own resolution to succeed is more important than any other one thing.* Abraham Lincoln

Once the preliminary concepts are formulated it is time to get clear on the why. Gary Keller, founder of Keller Williams Realty, says that the how becomes easy if the why is powerful enough. It is time to answer some questions of why you would want to take action on this concept.

- Who would benefit from your success?
- How would your life be different than it is today?
- How would things be if you never acted on this (or any other) idea?
- How would the lives of your loved ones…spouse, children, community…be blessed by your success?
- Most important of all, how would it make you feel to arrive at that place where your inspired goals were attained?

OBSTACLES

> *A company must be big enough to admit its mistakes, smart enough to profit from them and strong enough to correct them.* Bill Gates

Top Coaches Share Their Personal Action Strategies

Jim Rohn is one of my favorite business trainers. He is a contemporary to the well known speaker, Zig Ziglar. Both of them are constant sources of wisdom and I love the way that they express the realities of life. Jim tells how important obstacles are in achieving success. If you were to go onto a football field, grab a football and run to the end zone – have you really made a touch down? It is the obstacles that make the sport of football. Without the obstacles, there is no game.

In every story of inspiring people you'll find an underlying history of an underdog. Martin Luther King, Jr was imprisoned for walking over a bridge in protest. Do you think the jailer knew that someday our nation would designate a day each year in his honor? No, the jailer most certainly felt superior to the black man in his keeping and would have told him that he would be better off if he simply gave in to public pressure. Despite his apparent obstacles, King did not let that kind of opinion deter him from his goals. He set an example that will be remembered by the world for generations to come.

In fact, Dan Kennedy, a famous copywriter, calls the ability to overcome obstacles the "biggest success secret of all time". As he points out, this characteristic is a part of every person's success story. In the 1930s, Napoleon Hill's famous book, *Think and Grow Rich,* drilled in the need for this precursor to success. You will find it in successful athletes, coaches, business owners, inventors, sales people, parents and just about anyone who is known for their achievements. The one quality that all these people share is the ability to recover from adversity.

Everybody fails on their way to success. There are no exceptions. Try to find one highly successful person who hasn't failed. In fact, I venture to say that most have experienced more failure than success. Look at any book about success and you will find a discussion about the necessity of overcoming obstacles.

Let's be frank about the number one obstacle you will face. It is the obstacle of well-meaning friends and relatives who second guess your efforts. I have never seen statistics on this phenomenon, but I would suspect that every successful person in every field has had at least one person whom they love make discouraging comments about what is possible on the way to the goal. When someone you care about wants to save you from failure, it stings. But you must silently say, "I will give no space in my mind to your negative thoughts", and go on becoming a success. This loved one will be your biggest champion when you begin accomplishing your goals.

You may have heard this illustrative story about an old man, a boy and a donkey. Please excuse the punch line at the end and don't be offended.

Once there was an old man, a boy and a donkey from a small village that started on a journey to the big city. As they began, the old man led and the young boy rode the donkey. As they passed some passers-by commented about how wrong it was for the old man to be walking while the young, able-bodied boy was riding. After thinking about it, the boy and the man traded places.

Very soon, another group of people remarked, "What a shame. He makes that little boy walk. Thinking that "they" knew what was best, the old man and the boy decided that both would walk. Still, another group of people laughed at how stupid it was for both of them to walk when they had a decent donkey. So they both rode the donkey for a short while.

Now they passed some other people who rebuked them for putting such a heavy load on the poor donkey. Seeing only one way to appease the people, the old man and the boy picked the donkey up and carried him along the road until they came to a bridge. As they were crossing, the bridge swayed only slightly. The boy and the old man lost their grip – the donkey fell into the river, broke his neck and died.

The moral of this story: If you try to please everyone, you might as well kiss your ass goodbye!

We all love funny stories. But when they illustrate something as prevalent as the folly of trying to please others, it is time to really sit up and listen. Expect people to second guess your plan and you will be prepared to recover quickly when an obstacle shows up. Now, let's take a look at the final ACTION step.

NEVER GIVE UP!

There are many paths to the top of the mountain, but the view is always the same. Chinese Proverb

Let's recap. First, you devise a way to record all your ideas and to assess their merits. Once you feel you have found a viable concept that reflects your core competency, you visualize already having accomplished the goal with clarity and purpose. In order to further your clarity, you create a timeline with as many of the steps as you can imagine being required and place those items on a calendar. Now, use the power of why. Determine the cost of living a mediocre life when compared to the rewards for you, and for those around you, when you succeed. Prepare for obstacles. You cannot avoid them. Now, the only thing left is to be relentless.

Persevere. Of course, you would rather have an inspirational life without being the underdog and facing the reality of obstacles. But it simply does not happen that way. At times you will feel stuck. Being stuck kind of sneaks up on you when you least expect it. You simply drift into doing a little bit less today…then this week…it doesn't really feel bad at all. Then you wake up one morning and realize that you are way off your target. You have a reduction in problem solving skills. Your hope for the future is in jeopardy. You may suddenly feel fear.

When you have gotten off track, go back and review the five steps you have created for ACTION. Move toward your inspiration and you will be rewarded with more energy, focus and excitement. Take one step today and another tomorrow and don't stop. BE RELENTLESS!!!

I wish you an impassioned life of success. Enjoy the journey!

About Kathi

Kathi Frank has been a real estate leader since 1975. In 2006, she trained with Coach Institute. Now she has combined her skill of serving real estate buyers and sellers with her coaching ability. The result is a ground breaking course designed to enable real estate agents to work more effectively with the internet-enabled client.

Scheduled to be released in March 2008, this course will be delivered in diverse media. Combining tele-seminars, internet learning tools and a comprehensive workbook, students will benefit in a way that fits their own lifestyle. With the demands of the real estate profession, infinite flexibility will be honored.

Agents can expect to double their commission income as a result of this training. They will learn how to coach rather than sell; speak in a whole new language to these newly information-rich clients; and offer their essential knowledge based on the reality of real estate transactions. They will see that it is simply a matter of implementing an effective (coaching) language that serves this new breed of buyer and seller.

Prior to entering the business of coaching, Kathi spent more than 20 years in the real estate field. During that time she served in many capacities for the Women's Council of Realtors including local chapter President, Texas District Vice-President, and on several national committees. Frank has authored dozens of articles for the national magazine, *Communiqué* as well as several state trade magazines and a monthly newspaper column.

Contact information:
Kathi Frank
Kathi@KathiFrank.com
www.KathiFrank.com
www.TheWoodlandsConnection.com
www.The-Woodlands-Real-Estate.com
www.ConvertInternetLeads.com
Toll free (800) 448-2788

Move Your Life, Career and/or Business to the Next Level

By Laura Rubinstein, CHT

My corporation name is Transform Today. I specialize in supporting high-performance people to transform their bodies, business and relationships. Throughout this section, I will share with you some of my personal action strategies I use in the transformation process with clients and my own life.

These personal action strategies will allow you to cultivate your personal power and create anything you desire in your life. I mean anything. Whether you want a great relationship, ideal career or more peace, you are in store for the personal action strategies that you can use to create this in your life.

Transformation

Humans are full of paradoxes. We resist change and we get bored or "in a rut" when we are doing the same things over and over. The society we are acculturated into promotes succeeding at higher and higher levels. If you haven't recognized this yet, this can feel like a lot of pressure.

Transformation has become a buzzword in the world of self-help and has various interpretations. For the sake of clarity and effective use of this report, I will share my personal definition of transformation.

> **Transformation**: A process of taking responsibility for and causing an unpredictable outcome that has positive impact in your life, the lives of others and/or the world.

These personal action strategies will assist you in creating your world one of positive transformations.

The Key to Transformation is Knowing Yourself

The degree to which you will be able to identify and implement effective personal action strategies is directly related to the level you are willing to know and honor your Self. Let me explain. If you don't know what you want, what you like, what you need, what you feel, then you will wind up living at the effect of the circumstances of your life. In other words, you make decisions based upon what the cultural norm says you "should" do and the ideas of others rather than what will make you most fulfilled. If you know what you want, feel and need but are not willing to honor that, you will most likely feel powerless.

My personal action strategies are therefore based in both knowing and honoring yourself. Honoring yourself means taking the actions and making decision s that are in alignment with your highest good and what will bring you true fulfillment. Knowing yourself will help you determine what is for the highest good.

Here are some coaching questions that will help you get to know yourself more deeply.

- What's important to you?
- What are you feeling?
- Is there a message underneath this feeling?
- What do you need?
- What do you want for yourself?
- Where do you want to have a positive impact?
- What are your gifts and talents?

Accepting Yourself

Once you know about yourself, it is imperative that you accept these things. Trying to "change" yourself is often **not** the best personal action strategy.

One of the most damaging things, the "self-help" and coaching industry has done to people is to encourage them to "work on their weaknesses." I would like you to accept your so-called weaknesses and focus on your strengths. When you focus on the positive impact you want to have while embracing that with which you have been gifted, your decisions will be clearer. If you spend a significant amount of your time trying to work on your weaknesses and improve yourself, you may be cheating yourself out of valuable time of contributing from your strengths. Consider how you can work more fully in your strengths.

I realized that traditional studying to achieve degrees was not a strength of mine. I realized that I learn best from mentors and trial and error. I've fully accepted that I am not good at academic achievements.

Now instead of feeling bad about that or feeling like "I should" be a scholar, I have chosen to **trust**. I trust that it is not for my highest good that I be an academic achiever. With the acceptance of this I am free to focus on what I enjoy and am good at. I would also like to clarify that I love to learn. So this is where knowing yourself is really important. Since I love to learn and I'm not an academic whiz, I did not "give up" learning. Instead, I choose to learn in experiential environments instead of an academic one.

You never need to "give up" that which you enjoy. What you want to give up is the expectation that you "should" be a certain way. Instead of "shoulding" on yourself, try cultivating the best of you. Create the circumstances that allow you to thrive in.

Here are some coaching questions that will help you increase your self-acceptance:

- What are you resisting about yourself?
    - Can you give up resisting it?
    - What if it's best that things are the way they are?
- What "lemons" can you make "lemonade" out of?
- What can you appreciate about yourself right now?

Focus on Your Strengths

When you begin to let go of expecting things from yourself that are not true to your authentic make up, you have time and energy to focus on your strengths. This does not mean that you abdicate responsibility for things you are not good at if they are imperative to your physical, mental or financial well being. Rather, you delegate that which you can have others do and get support in accomplishing the other things.

Make a point to notice what you do well. Note those things that you take for granted. Do you make people laugh? Are you a good conversationalist? Do you understand people's feelings before they do? Can you read fast? Notice the things you do with new eyes and ears. Imagine an alien who just landed on the planet is watching you. What do they see? When you become aware of your gifts, talents and natural tendencies, you can then maximize them. If you take them for granted or discount them, they will be underutilized and you may walk around feeling like you don't know your purpose when it's right in front of you.

When you are clear of the gifts you've been granted, the personal action strategy is to be of contribution to others. Remember that being of contribution to others includes taking care of yourself so that you are in a position to be that contribution.

Here are some coaching questions that will help you focus and capitalize on your strengths?

- What do you do well?
- What comes naturally to you?
- What do others seek you out for?
- What do you enjoy doing that you feel like time passes too quickly?
- How can you use your gifts and talents to make the positive impact you want to have?

The people who have the hardest time getting into action are the people who have multiple talents or are good at everything. If you are one of these people, I recommend that you choose a few talents to focus on maximize. Choose the talents that can make the biggest contribution with right now.

Get Support for Your Authentic Expression - Mastermind Group

Now that you know what your strengths are and the positive impact you want to have in the world, you may find there is a gap between where you are, your talents and creating the positive impact.

Create a team of people, who believe in you, encourage you to bring out the best of you and create a life of joy. Find people in your life that can be your cheerleaders and believe in you no matter what.

We are placed on this earth with billions of other people; I think it's time to start co-creating. Knowing the gaps that need to be filled, seek out the pieces that will

Identify the support you need. Associate with others who encourage your happiness - not pressure you to meet their expectations or put you down.

Here are some coaching questions that will help you establish your support teams:

- What physical help and emotional support do you need?
- Who do you know already who can help or who knows others?
- What resources are available?
- Who do you want in your master mind team?

Self Compassion

Through this process of getting into action and moving through the ups and downs of everyday life, you can empower yourself, if you are compassionate with yourself.

When was the last time you said to yourself, "I am doing great" or "I am a kind, loving and wonderful person" or "I am beautiful and lovable" or "What I am feeling is perfectly ok?" Giving yourself deep understanding and generous love is the MOST IMPORTANT PERSONAL ACTION STRATEGY there is. When you cultivate more love for yourself, you have more to give. You can move through dark feelings and times quickly. You will also be happier and experience inner peace. From this state you are much more creative, energized and productive.

Here are some coaching questions that will help you cultivate self-compassion:

- What is your self talk?
- What can you say to yourself right now that is kind and loving?
- Every feeling you have is to be honored. What are you feeling?
- When you're upset, find out what need has not been fulfilled?

Practice Compassionate Communication

When you know who you are, you are in touch with your own feelings, and you are compassionate with yourself, you can connect with others more compassionately. Your communication comes from a place of taking responsibility for yourself on all levels. When people begin to communicate compassionately, they take responsibility for their feelings, for what they want and for honoring others as well.

Compassionate communication involves being authentic and vulnerable. There is no guilt, shame, blame or judgment coming from you. Others may have that in their communication and if they do you treat it with compassion. You can do this now because you are practicing compassionate communication with yourself.

If they get upset, it is mostly because a need of theirs isn't being met. Have compassion. Speak in terms of "I." The other day my landlord had agreed to put up a fence between my patio and my neighbor's for more privacy. When the handyman got there, he was going to encroach on three feet I wasn't expecting. Now I could have said, "You are encroaching on my patio and you need to move." Instead I said, I need the space for a swing we are putting in. I wasn't expecting that I misunderstood the location it was being placed." Did you notice in all of these later sentences I never used the word "you?" That is a technique for practicing taking responsibility. I didn't hurt anyone's feelings, judge anyone or make a demand because I took responsibility for the misunderstanding. In the end we compromised and each gave one and a half feet.

I was clear that I wanted more space. I didn't get distracted by what someone else did or didn't do. My focus was on what I wanted, not whether I was right or they were wrong. This is an important factor. When in relationship with others, being right is a very useless point to achieve.

When compassionately communicating it may be important to make a request, be sure to be clear that you are making a request and not a demand. You must be willing to hear no, otherwise it is a demand.

Here are some coaching questions that will help you practice compassionate communication:

- What can you take responsibility for?
- What specifically do you want?
- Who do you need to make a request of?

Cultivate More Joy

In this busy world we sometimes forget to enjoy ourselves. Creating joy is **not** a result of solving problems. You can have a lot of problems and still experience joy in your life. Problem solving only brings on more problems to solve.

The personal action strategy of cultivating more joy is imperative to the creative process. Joy is an experience of being in the flow of positive energy. Being in this positive energy flow typically doesn't happen by chance. Rather it happens consciously. You can up your joy in any moment you choose.

If it's a sunny day and you take a moment to appreciate the warmth of the sun and the blue sky and the fluffy white clouds, you will have had an experience that is available to anyone but must be chosen. It takes some practice and creativity. It does not take money or special circumstances. You can be joyous right now. The choice is yours. I highly recommend making that choice.

This personal action strategy will bring more fun, love and happiness into your life.

Here are some coaching questions that will help you up your joy:

- What's important about being joyful to you?
- What do you enjoy? List 50 things.
- What can you feel joyous about in your life right now?

It is my wish for you that you take these personal action strategies and use them merely as ideas for creating your own. Live joyfully. Love Deeply. Create Magic In Your World.

Top Coaches Share Their Personal Action Strategies

About Laura Rubinstein, CHT

Laura Rubinstein is a Master Leadership Coach, Hypnotherapist, www.WomeninJoy.com Community Founder and Marketing Consultant. She works with business owners and women to create more profits, more connections and more clarity and focus. Laura has been in business for herself for over fifteen years, specializing in business development for small business owners across the US and Canada. Additionally her six years in corporate management, extensive coach training and study with marketing and relationship gurus helped Laura to develop her true gift - coaching people in aligning their passions with their work and attaining goals.

In addition to working with private clients, Laura facilitates a variety of life changing programs including *Become A Man Magnet in 3 Simple Steps* and *Creating Juicier Relationships-Journey to Feminine Power* workshops. She is the author of *Transform Your Body In The Mental Gym^{TM}*, the *90-Day Body Transformation Program* and *Feminine Power Cards*.

Laura is dedicated to inspiring people to live their lives authentically with power, passion and fulfillment. Early training includes her earning an engineering degree from Vanderbilt University. Laura combines analytical skills, interpersonal wisdom and creative problem solving abilities to make her workshops, coaching and hypnosis programs highly effective.

Working with Laura is a journey to unleashing your authentic power and creating a life filled with harmonious relationships, true success and more joy.

Laura can be reached at Coach@TransformToday.com if you want to:

- Align your work with your passion,
- Transform your body and/or
- Tap into your feminine power and create great relationships

Other work by Laura includes authoring of *Transform Your Body in the Mental Gym*™ and the *Feminine Power Cards*.

Contact Information:
Laura Rubinstein CHT
Coach@TransformToday.com
www.WomenInJoy.com
www.HeartCenteredWoman.com
www.TransformToday.com
www.GreetingCardAssistant.com
(619) 293-3353

My Top 10 Motivational Strategies

By Lisa Smith, *MHT, NLP, CC, CCE*

What *is* motivation? The *American Heritage Dictionary* gives this definition: *the emotion, desire, physiological need, or similar impulse, to act.* The two key words here are EMOTION and ACT. Without emotion, there is no action. Without action, there are no results—no change, no growth. Although change can sometimes be fearful, as human beings we seek out newness and variety (at least on occasion). But if we keep *doing* the same thing, we keep *getting* the same thing (Action = Results).

I often hear my clients say, "I guess I'm just lazy" when they're not taking action on something. Laziness is a word that gets carelessly tossed around when people aren't willing to look at what's going on inside them. I don't believe people are *lazy*; I think they are just *unmotivated.* They are stagnant (lack of action) and unemotional (lack of emotion). Since we act out of emotion, not intellect, just "telling" yourself to do something or relying on force of will ("willpower") is inconsistent, ineffective, and frustrating. Remember the definition above. Thoughts backed by strong EMOTION create ACTION. It's estimated that we have about 60,000 thoughts a day, but we don't act on all of them. We act on the ones that have emotion behind them (which can be consciously or unconsciously stimulated).

Emotion creates energy and, as we learned in science class, energy creates motion. The emotion can be *pain* or *pleasure* (current or anticipated), but either emotion can get you into action. Pain is an "away-from" or avoidance motivator and pleasure is a "toward" or reward motivator. Most people are "away-from" motivated, meaning they will be more likely to take action to avoid pain than to gain pleasure.

But this is not the best way to motivate yourself. It either doesn't last because eventually you've made enough change to not be in pain anymore and slack off from doing what you did to get away from the pain, or you take such drastic action to get out of the fire that it's too far the other way and not sustainable (the mind has a hard time maintaining extremes).

In either case, you will eventually move back to the fire until it becomes hot enough to move you out of it again and the cycle starts all over (also known as the "yo yo" syndrome, very common among dieters). Therefore, although *away-from* motivation strategies can initially be helpful, eventually you must begin to utilize *toward* motivation strategies to maintain your momentum and success.

Toward motivators are the "brass ring" on the carousel; the pot of gold at the end of the rainbow; the thing you anticipate having or feeling as a result of your efforts - a longer life, more energy, feeling better, buying what you want, traveling, more freedom and peace of mind, etc. They draw you like a magnetic force vs. shove you from behind. Forward motivators quicken your heart in excited expectancy and get your mind geared into creative thinking. The 10 strategies I'm sharing here are Positive Motivational Techniques with forward momentum. Using them will allow you to view your future as bright, large, and colorful and lift the clouds of doom and gloom.

A big misunderstanding about motivation is that you have to wait around for it to "hit you" or "bless you" with its presence. People wait for motivation to "come" to them. The techniques I'm sharing here are time-tested by myself and others. In fact, I bet that any of the times *you* were actually motivated into action you employed one of them.

Now, these things might be totally foreign to you or feel somewhat familiar. Either way, you'll still have to consciously practice them until you get better at them and your subconscious takes over the new way of thinking and responding. But the rewards are worth it! I encourage you to try each of them at least once. Keep the ones that work best for you and use them again and again. Pretty soon, you'll be **unstoppable!**

First and foremost, with all these techniques, be forward-motivated vs. away-from

Focus on what you *want* instead of on what you *don't* want; your subconscious doesn't know the difference. It only knows what you are focusing on and will create the conditions, energy, and perceptions that will match it. Study and apply the Law of Attraction.

1. **Chunk it down**
    Goals are best accomplished by breaking them down into small steps or small accomplishments (e.g., start by improving one meal a day, lose 5 pounds a month, have 5 fewer cigarettes a day, exercise every day for 5 minutes or every other day for 10 minutes). Marathon runners don't stand at the starting line thinking about the 26.2 miles they have to run. They train their thoughts to

the first mile marker. Once they get there, they focus on the next mile marker. The distance is broken down in their minds and they just keep focusing on the small goals, knowing that as each one is achieved, they will get there. Do the same with your goals, especially if they seem like a marathon.

2. **Visualize your goal on a daily basis**
Remember; thought backed by emotion creates momentum. Bring yourself to your ideal future in your mind. SEE, HEAR, and FEEL the goal as if it has already been accomplished. Imagine it in the present and infuse it with imagery, sound (internal dialogue, external comments or music representing the wonder of it), and what you would be feeling—physically and emotionally—for having achieved it. Make it as vivid and detailed as possible and really *live it* for a few moments.

You can also create a **vision board** to help you do this more quickly; this is one of my favorites and can be a lot of fun! Get a variety of magazines with lots of images and cut out pictures and words that represent the things you want. Paste them onto a large piece of poster board or into a blank-paged sketch book. Separate the images into categories (e.g., wealth and objects, career, family/relationships, health, etc.). Look at it every day to impress the images upon your subconscious mind and see how many of them you've manifested after a year. Add new things as you accomplish the old goals. For a more dynamic vision board, make it a movie on your computer via an affordable, easy-to-use downloadable program I sell on my website.

Anchor it
After you've done the vivid future pacing, and you're really filled up with the positive feeling of being there, do something unique that your brain can anchor that feeling to (e.g., touch your thumb and first two fingers together on your non-writing hand or say a

short positive statement out loud like "It is done!" or hear a tune in your mind representing this empowering feeling (such as the Rocky theme song, or touch yourself on the left shoulder). Whatever it is, make sure it's something unique that you wouldn't ordinarily do and that you engage it for about 15 seconds while you see/hear/feel the positive emotions of accomplishing the goal. When you want to get motivated, engage the anchor again. The more you do it, the stronger it gets.

3. **Change your internal dialogue (self-talk)**
How are you talking to yourself? Negative thoughts lead to negative action (or no action). Are you cheering yourself on, encouraging yourself, creating a "can do attitude?" Is your critical voice getting more air time? Change that negative dialogue into a supportive one. This takes diligence and practice. Weeds grow wildly and easily in the garden of our minds. Plant seeds of flowers and keep up with your weeding. Read *What to Say When You Talk to Yourself* by Shad Helmstetter or *Self-Talk for Women* by Elise Thomas Helmstetter for more help on this. You can also write down positive statements that relate to what you want to believe about yourself or accomplish, things like "Every day in every way I'm getting better and better" or "I am a magnificent being capable of great things" or "I am slim, healthy, and beautiful." Post them on the bathroom mirror, the refrigerator, your car's dashboard, as a screensaver on your computer - any place you'll see them several times a day. Say them out loud whenever you can (and say it like you believe it!). You can also record them onto a tape or CD to listen to as you do things around the house or drive your car.

4. **Establish an attitude of gratitude**
Keep a daily gratitude journal (at the end of the day, list all the things you accomplished or are grateful for that day) or start your day mentally listing the things you are grateful for or thanking God/the Universe/whatever higher power you believe in for the things/people/experiences in your life. Focus on what you *do* have,

not what you don't. After all, if you can't appreciate what you already have, why would you deserve more? Focus on plenty vs. lack and you'll maintain a positive attitude to keep creating more to be grateful for in your life.

5. **Find ways to make it fun**
Let's face it, it's easier to get yourself motivated to do something if there is the anticipation of enjoyment with it. Get creative. If you have to do housework, do it with the radio blaring your favorite dance tunes and shake your booty while you dust the furniture. Listen to music or catch up on the shows you've Tivo'd while you ride that exercise bike. Add something you enjoy doing before, during, or after the task you need to complete. As Mary Poppins piped, "A spoonful of sugar helps the medicine go down."

6. **Join or create a MasterMind group**
Napoleon Hill, who wrote about the secrets of the most successful people of his time (Ford, Rockefeller, Carnegie, etc.), discussed how these men were part of a MasterMind group that met regularly to brainstorm business ideas and support each other in their goals. The principle is that several people getting together can focus special energy on their efforts in the form of knowledge, resources, and spiritual energy by tuning in to THE mastermind—God, Universal Power, or whatever you want to call that all-powerful life force. Not only can you get different perspectives and help with your goals, but the group helps you create an accountability and consistent momentum by stating your action commitments and meeting regularly. The group members won't let you slack off or buy in to your excuses, just as you won't let them. I've been in several MasterMind groups over the years, including right now, and have always gotten SO MUCH MORE accomplished when I am. If you'd like more information about how find/form and run a MasterMind group, do a search on line try www.speakernetnews.com/post/mastermind.html or read about

it in books such as *Think and Grow Rich* by Napoleon Hill or *The Success Principles* by Jack Canfield.

7. **Don't try to do it perfectly**
   Many people put off starting something until they have the "perfect plan" in place or wait for the "perfect time." They try to figure out all the variables beforehand so they don't "make a mistake." Well guess what - life is largely unpredictable. Timing is rarely ever "perfect" and you can't know all the variables of anything because we live in a cause-and-effect world. Taking action creates an effect that is sometimes different than what we anticipate. Life is a series of events and feedback. We can learn from *every* experience, whether we deemed the outcome of that experience as "good" or "bad." In fact, we often learn more through our failures than we do from our successes (there is no failure, only feedback). And who's to say that what you came out with wasn't guiding you perfectly to the resources, circumstances, or experiences that were just what you needed to get where you wanted to go? "Anything worth doing is worth doing poorly at first," so just *begin*. See what comes up next and make your best move from what you know *now*. The rest will come as you need it.

8. **Keep a schedule or routine**
   Flexibility is necessary when trying to accomplish goals, but so is structure. It's hard to stay focused and motivated when your world is unstructured or chaotic. Having a routine for your time and activities allows you to have a sense of balance and know where you have opportunities to work on your goals. Your mind gets overwhelmed when there's too much to consciously think about all the time. A routine also creates a sense of security that allows you to feel more comfortable in venturing out into the "unknown" by knowing you have something familiar to come back to when you feel a little shaky or scared. It's like a child learning independence—they take a few steps away from the parent but

come back for brief times in between to reconnect and become "brave" again.

9. **Don't go it alone**

   There are a variety of ways to get others to support you in your journey:

   Join a MasterMind group (see #7 above)

   Find a positive, supportive buddy who you trust to help keep you on track and committed to your success - someone who has created the success you want or is good at encouraging others would be a good pick. Or find someone who has the same goals as you do, so you can motivate each other and even work together to get your tasks done.

   Hire a professional such as a hypnotherapist or life coach. Using a professional who is trained, skilled, and experienced in helping people succeed beyond their own limitations can propel you into success much faster than you can often do on your own.

   > **Coaching** is a professional service providing clients with feedback, insights, and guidance from an outside vantage point. A coach is a partner in helping you move past "stuck" states to accomplish more than you can on your own by helping to clarify goals, create a plan for accomplishing them, identify and remove obstacles, create accountability to keep moving forward, and encourage you to recognize and acknowledge your successes.

   > **Hypnosis** is the ultimate means of heightening motivation by programming your subconscious (reflective) mind to work in cooperation with your conscious (reactive) mind to achieve desired results more easily. Your thoughts and beliefs established in the past have created your results of today, and they will continue to create your future. If you want different results and to move past self-limiting patterns, you MUST

influence the subconscious to think differently. Hypnosis is the best - and often fastest - way to create a life by design, not default.

At Life by Design Coaching & Hypnotherapy I offer both services—sometimes separately and sometimes in conjunction with each other. Some situations and clients produce great results with just the coaching element and some require straightforward hypnosis. But a combination of services often yields the best results. I also incorporate other tools such as NLP, EFT, Core Dynamics, and nutrition education to best serve each client's individual needs and energy. Whatever you're trying to motivate yourself to do, let me help you. Visit my website at www.hypnocoachlisa.com and contact me for a free consultation or sample coaching session to see how hypnosis and coaching can motivate YOU!

Top Coaches Share Their Personal Action Strategies

About Lisa

Lisa Smith, MHT, NLP, CC, CCE is a Certified Master Hypnotherapist, Wellness Coach, and NeuroLinguistic Practitioner serving the Hampton Roads area of Virginia. She is a HypnoBirthing childbirth educator certified by the HypnoBirthing Institute and is Ordained as a Minister of Spiritual Healing. As a member of the National Guild of Hypnotists, Toastmasters International, and the Junior Chamber of Commerce, she is committed to service and continuing education, and is currently pursuing a Masters in Holistic Nutrition. She was a senior staff hypnotist and trainer with the Virginia Beach center of Positive Changes for 7.5 years. With over 11 years of education and commitment to helping people improve their health and well-being, she has conducted more than 8,000 hypnosis sessions and 3,000 coaching sessions, and maintains a following of satisfied clients (see Testimonials page).

Her life mission is to use her training and experience in change and growth techniques to help people create powerful lives filled with health and self-fulfillment.

At Life by Design, Lisa offers personalized service and attention. Using hypnotherapy, coaching, neurolinguistic programming, and other tools, she offers can help you lose weight, eat better, stop smoking, improve your health, manage or eliminate pain, clear fears/phobias, decrease stress/anxiety, prepare for surgery, deal with cancer, increase self esteem, improve your business, excel in sports, and much more.

She can work with you in person or over the phone in most cases. She would love to talk with you and allow you to experience or learn about her services with no cost or obligation.

Contact Information:
Lisa Smith MHT NLP CC CCE
lisa@hypnocoachlisa.com
www.hypnocoachlisa.com
(757) 631-9940

Inspired Actions

By Lori Smith

It is 3 am again, I have paced the living room, I have drunk waaay too many caffeine products, and this is not the first night. I had this great idea, get as many coaches as I could together and write a book. Awesome idea, the first two volumes turned out super. This one is different though; this one is the first one going to print. I don't know, it seems to be more surreal or maybe just scarier...

Sometimes as coaches we have a hard time admitting that we have weaknesses as well as everyone else. This, this is the one I have had trouble with. I just couldn't get my mind to calm down enough to actually sit down and write my chapter.

There always was something that seemed much more important to do, post articles on the blogs, send out the newsletters, even sending out "pep" talks to the other coaches working on the book. But I just couldn't seem to get started.

Now I could blame "writers block", but really I was writing for the blogs three or four times a week, at least four newsletters, nope it wasn't writers block. I could blame the fact that I am too busy; I do work on a training and documentation contract as well as my coaching practice and spearheading this project. But just last weekend I sat around in my robe watching movies, just because I felt like it. Nope, "busyness" is just another excuse.

What about family? Well, let me tell you about that. One ex-husband, four teenagers between 15 and 19, cats, tanks full of fish and an AWESOME boyfriend (well he puts up with all of that, doesn't he?). Now I could tell you stories... But then I would be using it for an excuse again. I could spend half the night telling you about all of them (and I did but decided it didn't add much to the chapter so I removed it). I guess I'd better get to the point before you all fall asleep reading this; I had to come up with an Inspired Action Plan in order to move all those things that could get in my way aside to make room for all the greatness that will come from completing this little task and turning it into something great!

Here are the Inspired Actions that I used to not only get this chapter written, but to change my coaching practice and my life (really, it truly did change my life).

Inspired Actions is a phrase used by Abraham Hicks in the book *The Law of Attraction The Basics of the Teachings of Abraham*. When asked the question "How does hard work or physical action fit into your creative equation?" Abraham responded, "If you think your creation into being and then follow through with inspired action, you will find your future ready and waiting for you to arrive, and then you can offer your action in order to enjoy the fruit of your true creative power instead of incorrectly trying to use your action to create."

That one sentence jumped out at me like it was written only for me. To me it was the biggest impression that the Law of Attraction teachings has created. I have read all the books, watched all the movies, I understand the concept of thinking things into being. I have been a huge believer in "higher vibrations" since, well as long as I could remember. I have used and experienced the Law of Attraction before I even knew what the heck it was, but growing up in small town rural Canada, it was hard work all the way. Farmers and tradesmen, working from dawn to dusk; it was the way of life. This has been my hardest hurdle to overcome. Side tracked again… you can see why I need a system to keep me moving in the right direction.

Step one. Know what you want.

You would think that would be the easiest, but it isn't really. There are a couple of things that get in the way of finding out what YOU really want. Other people's expectations for instance, I am sure there are many people out there that can tell stories about how they picked their college major or their trade based on family pressure. "No one from our family has ever been a doctor/lawyer/accountant" or "Everyone in the family has been a soldier/police officer/plumber," when really all along you wanted to be a science teacher or scuba instructor.

The next thing and I believe the biggest issue - Self Confidence. You simply don't believe that you deserve to have nice things or have amazing adventures. Lots and lots of people have stories, stories of their lives and reasons that may stop them from moving forward. There are a lot of people wasting precious time, feeling like a victim and not looking to create better things for themselves. Granted, it is a lot easier said than done. It takes an enormous amount of courage to give up the baggage that becomes so comfortable for us, because we know it, rather than moving into an unknown better place.

Sometimes, you make a plan, you move toward the goal, you are very successful and then you look around and realize you definitely do not want to be here. Really it is not the end of the world;

this one is easy to deal with. You already know what it feels like to succeed. Just pick a new goal and work towards that one. Sometimes you really can't tell if you will like the feeling you get when you make your goal, until you are there. Aren't you glad that we live for 90 to 100 years that gives us soooo much time to try many different things, test them out, and see what we like?

There are many different methods to search for, open yourself up to, grab on to what you really, really want from your life.

Meditation

Meditation describes a state of concentrated attention on some object of thought or awareness. It usually involves turning the attention inward to a single point of reference. Meditation is often recognized as a component of eastern religions, where it has been practiced for over 5,000 years. Different meditative disciplines encompass a wide range of spiritual and/or psychophysical practices which can emphasize development of either a high degree of mental concentration, or the apparent converse, mental quiescence. The word meditation comes from the Latin *meditatio,* which originally indicated every type of physical or intellectual exercise, then later evolved into the more specific meaning *contemplation.*

Or, more simply put "meditation is the practice of quieting stresses to the mind by use of sitting and breathing techniques." Meditation can allow us to quiet our minds long enough to actually hear that quiet inner voice telling us what we want and need to be successful. Some people find this something that is very easy to do, others learn to be successful over a period of time, and still others never really get the hang of it. It is a good thing there are many ways to find ourselves.

Top Coaches Share Their Personal Action Strategies

Physical Actions

In the movie *Point Break*, Keenu Reeves' character, Johnny Utah, must learn to surf as part of his undercover assignment as a FBI agent. In one scene a boy of maybe 15 tells Reeves' character that "surfing's the source man... swear to God" while the line might be a bit unrealistic coming from a 15 year old, the point is valid. Many people use physical activities, surfing, running, biking, to calm their thoughts long enough to hear what their inner voice is really saying. Some of my best decisions were made during my 16km bike rides home every night after work. There is just something about sweating that helps you think more clearly.

Vision Board

Another technique that works really well and I have a ton of fun doing is a vision board. This is another really simple, simple process you need is a stack of pictures, a 4x4x1/4 plywood or cork board, scissors, tape/glue. Start with some really cool magazines, either House and Home or Budget Traveler, maybe you are totally into cars, boats or motorcycles, maybe all three. I have even printed things from the web that I really, really want.

1. Cut out pictures you want
2. Glue them onto the board
3. Hang up the board in a place where you can study it daily

Mine is hanging right behind me in my office space. I have actually one I created for a mountain lake retreat that I want and a second for some travelling that I want to do.

Technicolor Vision

Okay, so maybe you aren't into meditation or physical things; maybe you are a deep thinker or writer. There are still many ways that you can get to the bottom of what you really, really want. You can start with what my Coach and Mentor Terri Levine calls "a Technicolor vision." In this exercise you think about your perfect day, starting from the time you open your eyes in the morning until the time you go to bed at night. Write down every single, tiny detail: from what you see, what you smell, what you do, when you do it, who you do it with. Don't leave out a thing. Describe this day in the minutest detail, without leaving one thing out. I think that it is a great practice to do this every few months, to make sure you are moving in the same direction still, or maybe you have changed your mind about some things. Keep the picture clear in your mind, by reading it regularly.

Step two. Have Faith.

Another great book that has made a huge impact on me has been Napoleon Hill's *Think and Grow Rich.* In the book Hill describes a philosophy for gaining riches. He refers to money, but really it can be interpreted as whatever YOU believe is riches, whether, whether it is money, relationships, a lifestyle or a combination of all of them.

The first step Hill describes is Desire which we already addressed in the first Step "Know what you want." The second step Hill describes is Faith, the definition being "visualization of and belief in attainment of Desire (what you want)."

Many people will say, you need to visualize and feel your goals becoming reality, but Faith is more. Faith knows. And I mean deep down in your core, without a doubt, without a fear, without a second guess, that your goal will happen.

Have you ever had this happen to you? You are having a discussion with a family member, you are telling them with great enthusiasm what your next project or goal, is you could go on for hours on the subject. Ten minutes into the conversation, said family member says "you can't do that" and proceeds to list at least a dozen reasons why you can't reach your goal.

Normally, a person would start to doubt. You start thinking, "maybe what that person said was right, there does seem to be a lot of negative things that could happen." And now you have just talked yourself out of moving forward on that goal. Even if you don't actually give it up, it will never be successful or bring you the personal satisfaction you thought it would.

With Faith, you simple say "thanks for sharing your opinion." You never give it a second thought and you move on to find a person or circle of people that will support you with the same enthusiasm that you feel. As Hill says *Faith is the 'eternal elixir' which gives life, power, and action to the impulse of thought… Faith is the only agency through which the cosmic force of Infinite Intelligence can be harnessed and used by man.*

Step three. Create an easy efficient environment.

Now you can use this for ANY tasks. I am going to use my personal business/relationship building as an example.

Having had the experience of being in the Information Technology world for a long time, I am very familiar with systems and processes. This in turn led me to think, why can't I have these systems and process in my personal and business life in order to manage the day-to-day tasks in an organized and efficient manner? That way I can focus on doing the really cool, fun stuff.

First, I identified the tasks that I believed will be essential to building my business. Yes, these things do change, but changing every five minutes will distract you. Pick a specific time frame to try the task. For example, I decided that writing articles was a task that I needed to do to build my business and I have committed to doing it consistently for six months, tracking the results to determine if it is working for me.

Now you want to turn this task into a habit, just like brushing your teeth, a habit that comes as naturally as having a shower. Here are some strategies to move there:

1. **Identify a trigger.** In order for a habit to be a habit, you need to have a trigger. For example, you might brush your teeth after showering - the shower is the trigger for the brushing. And you know you're going to shower each day, so you know you will brush your teeth.

    When do you want to do your habit? What do you do at that time of day, every day? If you want to do something weekly, is there a weekly trigger that could precede it? My personal trigger is my Outlook software; I have tasks set up at specific times on certain days, a popup reminder 15 minutes the before scheduled time. This allows me to wrap up what I am doing and prepare for the next task. This works for me because I spend 95% of my allotted work time in front of the computer. You really need to experiment with what works best for you.

2. **Focus on developing the habit**. Once you've identified the trigger, you have to do the habit every single time you do the trigger, without exception, in order for it to become deeply ingrained. Focus on developing that habit for one month. Make it something easy, as you are more likely to not do the habit if it is difficult. If you are only doing a task weekly, a month will not be long enough, do it for three months for this.

3. **Only focus on that one habit.** I've said this many times before, but if you are trying to establish more than one habit at a time; your focus will be diluted. It's much harder. If you're

good at developing habits, you can get away with two or three at a time. But most of us aren't good at it, so focus on that one habit, for a month. After the month, you can work on a new habit. This may seem difficult, as you probably have a bunch of habits you'd like to adopt, but think long term: after a year, you'll have 12 great new habits!

4. **Journal it.** If the habit is important, you should Journal it. Make the Journal easy, and do it immediately after the activity. Don't put it off. This will make the habit more deeply ingrained.

5. **Report it to others.** Tell others you are going to do this habit for a month, and then report to them daily. If others are expecting your report, you will be more likely to stick to it. The more public pressure you put on yourself, the better. Put it on your blog, or join an online forum or some other group, have a coach, or email all your friends and family each day.

6. Once it's ingrained, you don't need a list. If a habit is firmly ingrained, and strongly attached to its trigger, you won't need to put it on your task list or any other list. You will just do it once the trigger goes off. And that's the payoff: good habits, without any of the thinking.

I have been able to successfully add to my business by building tasks and turning them into simple and easy habits. I write in my blogs at least twice a week, this happens now very easily and only gets missed if I am out of town. Next on my list is submitting one article per week to an article directory. Once I have finished writing this chapter it will become my next priority.

Summary

Now let's put this all together. At the beginning of this chapter, I came right out and admitted this was the hardest project I have ever written. It was hard to get focused and it was easy to procrastinate. It was extremely easy to come up with "things" to interfere and distract me from the task at hand. Too much pressure, my head is going to explode!! Okay I think I have been taking drama lessons from my kids.

The real problem was my lack of confidence that I actually had something important to write that people might not want to read. So I got in the way of myself and turned a few hour tasks into weeks of worrying really for nothing.

So here is how I did it. I put the bottle of Coke Zero down, traded it in for some White tea. Turned on some Jazz music, kicked the kids out of the house and the boyfriend to his office. Scheduled into my Outlook two hours, three times a week for writing with a pop up reminder to tell me when it is time.

During my "writing sessions" I worked on several things. Really targeting the specific message that I wanted to share - Inspired Actions - things really don't need to be as hard as we human beings make them. Totally getting in touch with my inner voice and listening to the depth of knowledge that is already there. Walking is my physical activity of choice right now, crisp clear autumn days, allow for your thoughts to just start following while you are walking.

Journaling all of my ideas in a special book, red special cover and everything, allows for great ideas to start evolving around each other and connecting in interesting ways. Definitely interesting feeling the Law of Attraction working on my ideas, a thought sparks a internet search, an internet search sparks a idea and the circle just keeps going.

Last but not least Faith, I have 150% complete faith that this project is going to be a success, I can see each and every coach impacted by the tremendous experience in participating and the outstanding value that each reader will gain from reading this book. As long as one person reads my chapter in among all the other great chapters written by the most amazing Top Coaches from around the world, I will feel privileged to say that I am part of this group.

About Lori

Lori Lynn Smith is a LifeStyle Coach and CEO of Foundation Coaching Group Inc.

Supporting Holistic Professionals Passionately create Meaning and Purpose in their New Businesses. My Mission... Inspiring Meaning, Passion and Purpose in your new Practice! I am on a mission to Create a Leading-Edge Coaching Community that will facilitate the creation of meaningful, successful and profitable practices for over 100,000 Holistic Professionals.

If you are a Holistic Professional this community has been created for you! As the next few months pass we will be creating a community that is filled to the brim with tools and resources to create a successful practice.

Do I understand that you MUST find your Dreams, your Goals and your Passions... yes! Here I am turning my dreams, passion and purpose into a lifestyle that I love and enjoying every minute of the journey.

Contact Information:
Lori Smith
info@foundationcoaching.com
www.foundatingcoaching.com
www.topcoachesshare.com
toll free (800) 399-9610

Top Coaches Share Their Personal Action Strategies

The Amazing Journey: Coming out the Coaching Way

By Martyn A. Dell and Jo Romano

Introduction

This chapter is a peek into a coaching relationship between a coach and her client. We hope that people who read this chapter will:

- find comfort and inspiration in hearing one person's story and personal journey to finding her authenticity.
- realize that self discovery can happen in a moment as well as over time.
- find hope and solace in their personal crises and realize that there are people to help and support them through the crisis.

Before we begin the journey, we'd like to share with you part of an e-mail we received from Vicki Lennox of Emerging Swan Coaching, "Congratulations to both of you on a truly inspirational piece of literature. Martyn, I was so very moved by your willingness to put yourself "out there", to show your underbelly, so to speak, to bare your soul, honestly and completely. To recognize your fears and to work through them, triumphantly under Jo's expert guidance. You really have portrayed life, yourselves and coaching in the most glowing terms. I am so very proud of you both and what you've accomplished in reality and the reporting of it in your chapter."

Who are Martyn and Jo?

We are both Certified Comprehensive Life Coaches trained by The Coaching Institute. Jo was Martyn's mentor coach when she joined CI in November 2005. We continued our coaching agreement after Martyn's certification in November 2006 because it was mutually beneficial.

Martyn Speaks: In December 2006, I ran head-on into one of the biggest personal crises of my life. I had been hiding a big secret from myself and the rest of the world for over 30 years and it was about to explode.

On December 13, 2006, during a University of Masters Parenting class, Jo had Emmy Howe, a Diversity Specialist from Cambridge, MA, with her to talk about Sexual Identity and Gender Expression. I was really looking forward to participating but when the time came for me to speak, I froze. That never happens!

After the call, I criticized myself for freezing. I realized I couldn't hide my bisexuality any longer. I had kept this secret to myself (except for a couple of disastrous experiences) because I was petrified of telling anyone else. I worried that I wouldn't be loved or accepted. I worried that I would be hurt.

I made the decision to confide in Jo and never looked back. We have documented this amazing journey and we'd like to share it with you. It's separated by months so you can see the action steps we have taken to move me forward. Let's begin.

DECEMBER

Martyn Speaks: It was only natural for me to confide in Jo since I trust her implicitly. We'd already coached through other personal issues during our year together. I sent her an e-mail telling her that I was so far back in the closet that the coats were smothering me. I shared my hurt about my best friend telling me, it was a phase. Excuse me! Phases don't last 30 years!

Jo Speaks: I sensed the hurt that Martyn was feeling about the phase comment and told her that her friend "has not learned about bisexuality for if she had she would know it is not a phase and that that minimizes a very real part in [Martyn's] relationship with her [friend]."

I also sought to dispel Martyn's own myths about bisexuality. I told her, "being bisexual does not mean that you are any more sexual than any other person. Separate that out. Remember it is all complex. Separate the bisexual from any improper behaviors. Improper behaviors do not happen because of being bisexual; they happen because of lack of boundaries and emotional disturbances."

I asked Martyn some powerful, clarifying questions because I know that she is very perceptive about her inner thoughts and feelings. I asked her, "How easy or difficult was it to talk with your friends when the topic came up?", "What did you communicate about you?", "Were you empowering and sending the messages that Emmy was talking about tonight?", and "Any breakthroughs about honoring who you are with others?"

Martyn Speaks: I told Jo that I'm ready to emerge from the closet. I needed and wanted to honour myself by being honest about my sexuality. I expressed my hope that I would attract my ideal clients to me by living my authentic life and that I might possibly help teen girls who are questioning their own sexuality.

One of my consistent actions is to write a Reflection Journal for Jo to track my progress, the challenges I'm facing, how my spirit has changed, and any insights or breakthroughs that I make.

In my Journal for December 20, I wrote that I've felt the confusion and pain of hiding a big part of myself but I was in denial that it was even affecting me at all. My feelings for women would pop up sporadically but I would ignore them. I couldn't do it anymore. But I also felt the fear of coming out and what it would mean for my career and personal life. Then I questioned, "Is it anybody's business and can't I just stay in the closet and not rock the boat?" But that didn't feel right either. I was so confused!

Jo Speaks: During our coaching session on December 20, I encouraged Martyn to find support in her community. I knew she would be able to find lots of online resources easily but wanted to see her find offline support too.

We also talked about what it would feel like to come out and live authentically. I recognized Martyn's confusion and overwhelm and reassured her that she didn't have to decide this now. I stressed to her that this is a transition and to be gentle with herself.

Martyn Speaks: After our session, I felt supported and loved but I was still confused and very emotional. Jo knew this and wrote, "Thank you for sharing your feelings with me. I stand by you every moment. I stand right next to you with my hand gently on your shoulder, smiling in celebration of you and what is blossoming in you (with all the scary emotions). Be compassionate when you are in your depths of despair. I know you will be alright so please lean on my clarity and strength, which is really yours."

I started doing online research and ran into a YouTube video with Fred Phelps' daughter and a Fox newscaster. The hate and anger they were spewing at each other deeply upset me. I wanted to stay in the closet since it's safer there and I'd already been passing as straight for 30 years. But I knew it was getting harder to keep silent and another accidental slip of the tongue was possible.

I found a local Parents, Families & Friends of Lesbians & Gays (PFLAG) group but they hadn't held meetings for three months since attendance was low. Joanne, the PFLAG contact, provided me with some good information and advised me to do lots of reading. I headed to the public library and cleaned out their gay section."

Just after Christmas, Jo sent me an e-mail asking how I was doing. I told her that I'm feeling more positive and hopeful now that I've started to take action.

Jo questioned "What other ways can you come into your personal truth without coming out to people like mom, etc.? What needs to come together inside you that will pave the way to whatever is next?"

Jo reminded me that "We are all where we need to be and we are perfect today. And tomorrow more will be revealed. Go gently...it's the coach's way."

At the end of December I decided to put my own coaching practice on hold for the time being to focus on my authenticity. I gave myself permission to take this time to re-discover my sexuality. I have the coaching skills and Jo's support to guide me in my journey and ultimately my clients will be attracted to the whole, authentic me.

Jo Speaks: This was a perfect plan. I reminded Martyn that often when we have our commitments set on a specific goal, another one feels more relevant and immediate so we let go of the original goal and move toward the new one. I fully supported her in this decision.

Playwork for December: Jo assigns me action steps every session to move me forward. We call this Playwork. This month I was to begin examining my limiting beliefs around bisexuality. I started doing this by reading books from the library and analyzing how I felt about what that author was saying. I would ask myself "Is this statement true for me?" or "Does this resonate with me?" If it did, it would go on my list of truths. If it didn't, I would skip past it since it wasn't MY truth.

Jo also wanted me to search for online and offline resources to empower myself. I did a lot of Google searches trying to find the appropriate resources for me amongst all the dreck.

These were baby steps for me because I was still in crisis mode. When a client is in crisis, the experienced coach knows that the client has to be ready to move forward and will allow her the time to reach that point without prodding or pulling her. Jo's support allowed me to find my balance and start taking action fairly quickly.

JANUARY

Martyn Speaks: I started January off feeling grateful for having the coaching skills I learned from Jo and her support in dealing with my bisexuality. I was determined to start bringing more people into my Circle of Courage (as Jo calls it). My Circle of Courage consists of people I trust with intimate information about myself and trust that they will not harm me in any way. Obviously Jo is one of those people!

Top Coaches Share Their Personal Action Strategies

I decided who I wanted to come out to and on January 4, 2007, I told Jo that I came out to my friend Ann at lunch. I was ecstatic. I was very nervous but felt in control and that it was my choice to tell her. I knew that she would be supportive because we had already shared personal information. Now that I've called Ann into my Circle of Courage I feel amazingly free because I don't have to hide my bisexuality from her anymore.

Telling Ann was like pulling the plug in the bathtub. I came out to four more people during the next two weeks. It was a lot easier after the first one. All were very supportive albeit surprised because I had hidden this part of myself for over 30 years and I was an expert at it.

Jo Speaks: During our first coaching session of 2007, I helped Martyn explore the conflict she was feeling about not telling her mother of her bisexuality. We named her fears and examined whether they were the truth or not. I asked her, "Is it true that finding out about your bisexuality would actually kill your mom?" I could feel the shift of energy in her as she realized that wasn't the truth. I made a powerful request that Martyn list her truths to allow her to see which ones weren't serving her any longer.

I observed that Martyn was feeling pressure "to come out" to make herself honest and she agreed. I also reminded her that coming out is a process and that it is her choice, if and when she comes out, and that it will happen on her own schedule. I could feel her energy shift from frenzy to calmness and acceptance.

On her own, Martyn decided to use a coaching tool I introduced her to last year called a GROWTH Exercise (the format is below in the playwork for January). She decided not to tell her mother about her bisexuality. She felt comfortable with this conscious decision because it was not based on fear.

Top Coaches Share Their Personal Action Strategies

I requested that Martyn write possible responses to her mother if she accidentally finds out and Martyn wrote a very detailed transcript of her mom's possible emotions and reactions.

The day after our coaching session, I received Martyn's e-mail about coming out to her friend Ann. I was so proud of her. This was huge. She is such a beautiful person! I reminded her I was standing right beside her.

Martyn Speaks: I continued searching for resources in January. I found online resources but no support groups in London for my age group (late-30s). Then all of a sudden the resources poured in. I truly believe in the adage that when the student is ready the teacher will appear. I found a shop (Libido – Lesbian-owned), a social group (Adventurous Womyn of London – AWOL) and a local cable TV show (Today's Q). Now, I've lived in London for 20 years and I never knew these resources even existed.

I was really excited to find a zine called The Fence which is edited by a bisexual activist in Toronto. She wanted to create a safe place for women to express their thoughts and views about being bisexual. I promptly purchased a subscription.

Playwork for January: An expert coach, like Jo, will assign her client homework that allows her to take baby steps to quickly achieve success and gain momentum. To demonstrate this, Jo requested that I keep listing my truths to see which ones aren't serving me any longer. I continued adding to it until I had to organize it into 16 categories. I ended up with a pretty comprehensive view of my beliefs as they pertain to all aspects of my life (not just my bisexuality).

To move myself forward I completed a GROWTH exercise. This tool is an expanded pros and cons list that helps you examine your feelings and the outcomes you want from making a decision. The acronym stands for:

- **G** oal (What do I want?)
- **R** eality (What is my current state?/What's happening right now?)
- **O** ptions (What are the costs and benefits of the decision? - this is the pros and cons list)
- **W** ill (What I will do?)
- **T** eaching (What did I learn?)
- **H** abits (What changed?)

I answered the questions and created my chart for the costs and benefits of telling or not telling my mother. From this exercise I decided not to reveal my bisexuality at this point.

Jo also requested that I write a transcript of possible responses to my mother. I listed 12 possible reactions that I could get (i.e. anger, disgust, or confusion) and imagined what I would say to her in each case. Jo told me they were heartfelt, compassionate responses and that I'm a wonderful daughter!

To empower myself I continued searching for online and offline resources and after much Googling was able to find the resources I was looking for.

FEBRUARY

Martyn Speaks: I began February thinking I needed to market my coaching again. I was feeling lazy and self indulgent for taking a month off. I had colleagues at work questioning me about when I was leaving since they knew I was starting a coaching practice. At the same time I was still interested in my self exploration. It was internal and external pressure.

Jo Speaks: Martyn mentioned, during our February 6, session, that she was feeling pressure to start marketing again. I reminded her that coaching is about working on one goal at a time. Her goal changed and there's nothing wrong with that. I also helped Martyn examine her limiting belief that she was being lazy for wanting to do this self exploration now.

On February 14, Martyn and I reflected on how far she has come in the last year. We listed her achievements, discussed where she is currently in her coming out journey, and where she wants to go in the future. This is the Past, Present, and Future coaching skill and I love to use this with my clients to help them celebrate their successes and build upon the momentum for their future goals. Martyn has aced this skill!

Martyn Speaks: I told Jo I wanted a life partner so she requested I write a vision for love and intimacy for 2007. This was the first vision I wrote that I could actually feeeeeel. It was so vivid! I even recorded it to play it on my MP3 player. I also shared it with two other close friends besides Jo so the four of us could hold the vision for me more powerfully.

I wrote in my Reflection Journal for February 28 "Now that I'm coming out to people, I feel freer, happier, and more content. I think people are starting to see it. I am glowing these days!"

I thought I was handling my coming out journey very well but apparently not because I started having heart palpitations from an anxiety attack. I was so focused on coming out that I didn't stop to address the stress and fear I was feeling and my body reacted to it.

Top Coaches Share Their Personal Action Strategies

I strongly believe that we all have inner children inside and I realized I was neglecting mine. She was scared of what was happening to us. I wrote her a letter to apologize for neglecting her and to reassure her that she didn't have to hide our secret anymore. We could share our bisexuality. I told her that I would always be there for her. My heart stopped pounding!

I went to my first AWOL event on February 21. The Inspirational Discussion Group was amazing and I had a lot of fun. There were five of us, all lesbians except for me. I felt welcomed and accepted. Because I'm an introvert, I'm nervous in new situations but I felt comfortable there right away. Jo made some powerful observations of this meeting.

Jo Speaks: I noticed that Martyn separated herself from the others and wondered what that was about. She told me that it was preconceived notions she got from reading old library books that lesbians often resent and avoid bisexuals for fear that they will get left for a man. I cautioned Martyn to keep an open mind about the gay and lesbian community because it is her community too. Stereotyping gays and lesbians can be self deprecating.

Playwork for February: There were three major action steps I took this month: writing the letter to my inner child, writing my vision, and attending my first AWOL event. To write the letter, I calmed my mind and listened to what was in my heart. I reassured my inner child that I would not hurt her or neglect her again. By writing this letter I was coaching myself through the fear and the anxiety was relieved.

To be honest, I forced myself to go to the Inspirational Discussion Group because I was definitely stretching outside my comfort zone. Coaching is all about taking the baby steps to achieve success but sometimes big steps are needed. This was a huge step for me because it was my first foray into the lesbian community.

To write my vision for love and intimacy I picked a date one year ahead and visualized that day with my perfect partner. I incorporated the five senses plus my feelings into my vision and wrote what I saw. It was 9 pages long and took 6 days to write because it was so detailed. I recorded my vision with my free teleconferencing line (www.thebasementventures.com) and they turned the call into an MP3. I downloaded it to my computer and then onto my MP3 player. I then shared my vision with Jo and two other friends to gather the collective energy and make it more powerful. Jo often assigns me visions to write because they help me gain clarity into what I really, truly want in my life. It's a very powerful coaching tool.

MARCH

Jo Speaks: Martyn sent me the letter she wrote to reassure her inner child and I asked her to list the child's biggest fears (which, of course, are Martyn's). After receiving the detailed list, I requested that she identify what habits and patterns are blocking her for each statement (i.e. limited thinking, fear, victimization) and turn each around with a truthful, self preserving, and self celebrating statement. I also requested that she list 10 ways she can nurture herself and her inner child. Martyn developed some brilliant, nurturing, and honest statements for her habits and patterns and some simple ways of taking extreme self care to reduce her stress.

Martyn Speaks: March was a turning point for me when I realized that the most important people in my life now know I'm bisexual. I was comfortable with the idea of others finding out through my everyday activities. I'm not hiding my bisexuality anymore.

On March 10, I stretched out of my comfort zone again by going to my first gay bar, alone. It was a female impersonator show and fundraiser for London Pride this summer. The show was great but I was too shy to talk to anyone. I realized that coming out didn't change my dislike of the bar scene. I didn't like it when I was "straight" either.

Jo sent me an invitation to write a chapter for the Top Coaches Share project on power strategies. I wanted to write about my power of faith in myself and the Universe. During our coaching session on March 14, we talked about revealing my bisexuality in my chapter. I was concerned about putting myself out there.

Jo and I went through an oral GROWTH exercise during the session because I was still conflicted about including my bisexuality in my chapter or not. Jo suggested that I include it but not submit the chapter if I wasn't ready.

I shared the written chapter with Jo and another close coaching friend and they both thought it too revealing. I heeded Vicki's advice and cut out a good chunk of it before submitting it.

Playwork for March: Jo assigned me the playwork of examining my fears, labelling them, and then turning them around into affirming statements. The fears were very easy to write because I'm able to acknowledge my fears easily. To identify the habits and patterns that are holding me back I went through my coaching manual to put labels on them such as conversations of limitations or conversations of fear. To flip the fear around I thought about what I wanted. For example, one fear was not finding my place in the lesbian community. This was a Conversation of both Fear and Limitation. To flip it around I wrote "There is a place for everybody in the lesbian community. There is a great diversity among lesbians and all I have to do is be myself and I will naturally find the place I fit in."

To find the place I fit in, I stretched myself by going to the gay bar. I discovered that it was not the right place for me so it was a learning experience. I knew the right place was out there for me; I just had to find it.

Writing the chapter for Top Coaches Share was a major action step because it was putting myself out there in a major way. I was coming out to the whole world! Writing the first draft was easy. Hacking out chunks of it was difficult but I did end up with a better chapter.

APRIL

Martyn Speaks: I started feeling dread right after I sent the chapter in. I told Jo "I have an "uh oh" feeling in my stomach which is probably my inner child screaming in horror." I was in a state of panic and confusion. I thought I made the biggest mistake of my life but Jo wrote back, "You speak from the heart and you toned down the emphasis on bisexuality - which I think is good - even though your personal focus these days is discovering it. To the listener, it is just one thing in your life that describes who you are. It is not all you are."

I replied with, "Now that I've had time to think more about my chapter I feel better about it. I got some really good feedback from another coaching buddy about the final version which I sent to her. The only thing that would make me feel safer is to remove all mention of my bisexuality but then it wouldn't be authentic and that would feel worse. My bisexuality is part of my power, it's part of who I am, and I'm proud of it. I don't want to call it off. I'm feeling the fear and doing it anyway. I think my fears are just limiting beliefs. Is is really going to affect me if someone looks down on me for being bisexual? No! I'm here to please myself first. I'm not living my life to please anyone else."

The London Lesbian Film Festival was at the end of April and I was very excited. During our session on April 25, I told Jo that it felt like my debutante ball - I'm coming out to the lesbian community. We spent most of the session talking about my feelings and fears surrounding the event. I was feeling fat and self conscious. Jo said to go to my vulnerability, the place where I am most authentic and real, and honour myself as the beautiful person I am.

Jo Speaks: I could tell that Martyn was excited about the festival but obviously nervous too. I requested that she write a vision for how she wanted to experience the festival. Martyn wrote separate visions for each of the three days. They were beautiful, fun, excited, and all HER.

I also observed that I was hearing conversations of fear of the unknown. I requested that she do a Dump and Flip exercise to coach herself through her fears about the festival and write her self coaching statements. The instructions for this tool are below in the playwork.

Aside from the festival, I observed that Martyn had been distracting herself from thinking by doing so much. She became somewhat silent. I requested that she feel her authenticity. I also introduced the coaching principle that LESS IS MORE and I requested that she ponder what "less is more" means to her.

Martyn Speaks: I felt trepidation about the playwork that Jo assigned me on April 25 because I had fallen back into an old pattern of using "busywork" to keep myself distracted from feeling. This provided a barrier between my inner and outer experiences. Jo said it's time to stop letting others speak to me and let my voice have its own say. I owe this to myself and my personal growth. My foundation is getting stronger every day.

I had such a great time at the London Lesbian Film Festival. The movies were amazing! There were a couple of upsetting ones about rape but right after there was a hilarious one about four lesbian comics. One funny part of the night was when the MC asked the audience how many of us had cats and 3/4 of us put up our hands. I thought that was hilarious. Do you have to have a cat to be a lesbian?

Playwork for April: When Jo requested I write a vision for the festival, I decided to do separate ones for each day. Once again, I imagined the outcome that I wanted, how I would look and feel, and incorporated my five senses into them. The difference this time is that I set a timer for 30 minutes to write each one. I was demonstrating the "less is more" principle at Jo's request because she knew my vision for love and intimacy took me 6 days to write and she wanted me to simplify the process.

I completed a Dump and Flip exercise to calm my fears about attending the festival. This is an excellent tool to gain perspective on an issue. You take a piece of paper and fold it in half lengthwise. On the left-hand side you dump everything that is bothering you. On the right-hand side you flip it 180 degrees to make a positive statement. For example, I wrote "I haven't found my "style" in the gay community." and then I wrote "The gay community doesn't have a single style. There is great diversity and there is room for everyone."

MAY

Martyn Speaks: After Jo requested I listen to my inner voice, she sent me an e-mail stating 'My observation is that although you are reading lots of books and getting inspired and learning, the very act of reading the books is a distraction and a false energy pattern. Reading books is easy for you to do and it's a safe place for you. It is not a stretch for you to be reading books. Is this your truth?"

She wrote further, "Being with your vulnerability, noticing your deeper feelings when you are giddy, exploring habits and patterns that impede your vision and goals, and seeing your vision, feeling it, writing it, and speaking it - these are things that are very sacred. These are internal actions and quite often feel uncomfortable and more difficult because they do not require "doing" like reading a book - instead they require just being and reflecting. Does this resonate for you?"

It did resonate with me because reading is one of the patterns that I always return to. It protected me when I younger. I could always trust books not to abuse, hurt, or shame me. Reading allowed me to see that there was hope in the world - to make sense of the world and my place in it. I used books as a barrier between myself and the world.

It was only natural for me to read about gay, lesbian, bisexual, and transsexual (GLBT) issues but Jo was right. It was time for me to listen to my inner voice and let it shine forth. She made a very wise observation and now I recognize my false energy pattern.

On May 9, I mentioned to Jo about getting back into coaching. Jo thinks it's because I'm doing my inner work right now and it's really hard BEING instead of DOING. I'm to stick with the BEING. The fact that I question being ready means that I'm not and when I am ready I will know it instinctively.

In May, I met a man through the PFLAG-TALK mail list that I joined in January. The list isn't associated with PFLAG but does provide support for parents, friends, and families of the GLBT community. Steven was having a hard time dealing with his attractions to men and women. I provided support on the list and he e-mailed me privately. We struck up a mutually supportive e-mail friendship where I was practicing my coaching skills and he was getting a sounding board for his thoughts and feelings.

Coaching Steven inspired me to want to coach older GLBT people in coming out and living authentic lives. I realized that my coaching skills and Jo's support helped me come out and I want to provide support for other GLBT people. There is a definite need in London for coming out support groups for older adults.

My bisexuality didn't take a front row seat in May. I reached a point where I was able to provide support to someone else instead of just receiving it. You know you've nailed something when you can actually help someone else with it. Jo was able to coach me around other issues that were coming up in my life.

Playwork for May: The only playwork this month was to listen to my inner voice. To do this I had to make some changes to my usual routine. I stopped reading and listening to my MP3 player on the bus (I take public transit or walk everywhere) and reading during meals. It was difficult to do at first but it was a valuable exercise because I was able to gain clarity into my inner thoughts and beliefs. This allowed me to move forward in great leaps and bounds.

JUNE

Jo Speaks: I loved the idea for Martyn's new focus for her coaching practice. I thought of it a few weeks ago but didn't want to put pressure on Martyn since she was still discovering herself. I asked her when she knew and she told me that when she started supporting Steven it coalesced into a definite goal. Martyn sounded very clear and specific about what she wanted to do so I helped her narrow her niche to coaching GLBTQ (Gay, Lesbian, Bisexual, Transexual, and Questioning) people between the ages of 18 and 40. I asked what her first step would be and she said a Goal Planner since this is a brand new goal for her.

Martyn Speaks: On June 6, Jo and I did an oral Goal Planner (which I expanded after the call). It was enlightening because I realized I have the time, energy, and emotion to build this coaching niche but I'm lacking the financial resources. That could be a roadblock to success. Jo requested that I set some money intentions. I also wrote a new money vision.

On June 20, Jo used powerful observations to indicate that my debt needs to be dealt with before I coach GLBT clients. That was very difficult to hear. One of Jo's best qualities is that she provides a safe coaching space for me to express my hurt, sadness, and anger. She isn't afraid to ask the difficult questions that may cause upset feelings. Some sessions my intention is to not cry but the coaching is so powerful that sometimes I do and that's OK.

Playwork for June: It's pretty common knowledge that it's easier to achieve your goals when they are written down. The Goal Planner that I use helps me gain clarity around my goal. It states the goal desired, the reasons for it, how my life would change, and how I would be happier achieving the goal. Then the action steps and a timeline for them are listed. Resources (time, energy, emotion, and money) are listed next. The last section lists dates to measure progress and adjust the steps if required.

To set my money intentions I asked myself what I really, really want regarding my finances and listened for the answer. I listed 13 money intentions which were really short and long term goals. I used these money intentions to create my money vision. Once again, I confined myself to a 30 minute time limit for simplicity.

JULY

Martyn Speaks: Once again my goal changed. I'd made a lot of progress in coming out and now I needed to work on my finances to prepare for my new coaching niche. At the beginning of July, I joined an 18-week support group led by two of my coaching buddies and based on Joan Sotkin's book Build Your Money Muscles: Nine Simple Exercises for Improving Your Relationship with Money (www.prosperityplace.com/index.php). The purpose of the book and group is to change your relationship with yourself and others so that you can bring more prosperity into your life.

I discovered that money problems aren't about money itself. I had been fearful, confused, and repressed about my bisexuality for more than 30 years and this manifested in low self esteem, low paying jobs, and credit card debt. Now that I'm more authentic about my bisexuality the fear and confusion are gone and I'm ready to start dealing with my finances.

In her book, Joan writes, "While moving consciously through a significant transformation, people notice subtle changes occurring almost daily. A slight positive shift in attitude, for instance, might lead to a new thought that stimulates a more comfortable emotion and functional behavior, all of which can catalyze minor yet observable improvements in life circumstances. Over time, such incremental upgrades can amount to a major modification in life position. The same holds true in financial growth." This mirrors my coming out journey!

London Pride marked one of the top five defining moments of my life. It was especially sweet because it was Pride's 25th anniversary and my first! The 10-day event kicked off on July 20 with City Hall raising the rainbow flag for the first time since 1995 and I stood front row centre. Pride Literary Night was on July 24 and it was fantastic! I shook Michael Riordan's hand and told him how much his book Out Our Way meant to me.

The first night of the Pride festival weekend was on July 27. During the drag queen show one of the queens asked if there were any first-time attendees in the audience. I threw up my hand and was pulled up on stage. I came out to about 3000 Londoners and was known as the "Pride Virgin" for the rest of the festival.

Top Coaches Share Their Personal Action Strategies

If you read my chapter in the second volume of Top Coaches Share, you'll remember I don't believe in organized religion and hadn't set foot in a church for 30 years. I knew instinctively that I wouldn't be accepted there because I was bisexual. I had absorbed the message that homosexuality was a sin and that I was a sinner and God didn't love sinners. I rejected religion because it rejected me.

You'll find it ironic that one of the best parts of the weekend was the Pride Services at Metropolitan Community Church (MCC). They were very inspiring. I cried during the prayer which was about inclusiveness, acceptance, and love. I heard the message and accepted it as the truth. I felt so welcomed, validated, and nurtured. Everyone was so friendly. I got lots of hugs and was recognized again as the "Pride Virgin".

I believe in a higher power and would call myself an agnostic. MCC welcomes people of all faiths so I felt comfortable there. It was a very positive experience and I intend to go back. I've found a spiritual community that I feel comfortable and welcome in. I've been searching for my spiritual path since hitting my 30s but had to begin my coming out journey before it was revealed to me. I've found my place to belong. This is where I fit into my community.

Capping the weekend was the Gay Pride parade. I was naturally nervous about marching and thought about just going as a spectator but then thought "Damnit! No! This is my Pride (and my pride) and I'm claiming my place in it." Besides, how would it look if the Pride Virgin was on the sidelines.

To be surrounded by so many gays, lesbians, bisexuals, transexuals, and supporters was very heartwarming, affirming, empowering, and validating. There were people lined up on the street cheering at us and waving rainbow flags in support. We had cars honking at the intersections. It was a beautiful experience. There was only a very small contingent of protestors with nasty signs. I just blew them a kiss and yelled "We love you too!"

Pride was an amazing experience. It was fun, empowering, validating, enlightening, entertaining, and liberating. I am proud to be who I am! I'm part of the gay community, my community. I repressed who I am and who I am attracted to for more than 30 years. It feels exhilarating to finally be honest and authentic about who I love. That's my truth and I'm not afraid to say it.

Jo Speaks: I provided Martyn with powerful observations on patterns that are holding her back from becoming authentic. She has a special knack for self reflection and never shies away from delving deeper to peel away the layers to get at her truth. I wrote her, "It is difficult to look at our realities - even the ones we don't want to think or remember about. But isn't that what self reflection is all about. Peeling the onion or shall I say the flower petals back and going deeper ... Crying is also good because it is a very intimate thing to do."

I also wrote, "Thank you for sharing yourself with me. You are a beautiful person in ALL ways. A partner will be very lucky to share her life with you. Just notice when you feel like you are closing down, or to say it simply, feeling and being in your vulnerability. It's the best place to be, even if it does feel uncomfortable at first. You are changing and creating new ways, approaches to life, and relationships. One baby step is all you need to take today."

Playwork for July: The playwork for this month was more self directed because of the Build Your Money Muscles support group I joined. I was doing my actions steps for the program and sharing the results with Jo. My expert coach abides by the coaching principle that the client guides the session, not the coach. She let me run with it because I had the momentum going. She just had to hang on for the ride.

What's Next for Martyn and Jo?

More coaching! The coaching agreement doesn't end when the client has achieved his or her goal. The client and coach are always peeling back the layers of the onion in another area. They are delving deeper into the ocean and that's why coaching can last for years. When the client and coach are perfect for each other they move on to the client's next goal. We demonstrated this during the 8 months included in this chapter when Martyn's goal changed from marketing her coaching practice, to coming out, to working on her finances.

Martyn Speaks: I can say without a doubt that Jo has been one of the biggest influences in my life to date. Without the coaching skills that she taught me and the love and support she has given me over the last year and a half, I would still be in the closet. The sense of freedom I have now is immeasurable! Jo's warmth, compassion, encouragement, and humour are amazing to experience. She is not afraid to confront me about my limiting beliefs and help me examine my own truth. She encourages me to be in my vulnerability even when it is uncomfortable for me because that is where my authenticity lies. I can express myself fully to her without fear of judgment or criticism. I count her as one of the greatest blessings of my life! I look forward to many more years of coaching with her as we co-create to build my coaching practice.

Jo Speaks: Martyn is truly a beautiful woman, friend, daughter, lover of life and people, client, and coach. She is an ideal client for me because she is open to receiving new insights and breakthroughs that catapult her towards reaching her goals and vision. She takes baby steps, (less is more) simplifying her thinking and feeling, and playing with new approaches to old thoughts or patterns. She is a true believer in possibility and the power to create the life and work she loves. She is articulate, thoughtful, and not afraid (really) to stretch and revel in the gifts that present from such deep personal courage. She has strong coaching skills and instincts to "tune in" to others and is a stellar coach for all wanting to celebrate and explore who they are, what they want, what's getting in the way of what they want, and how they will achieve it. Martyn is loyal and steadfast to her clients and, as such, will attract her ideal clients thus making it a win for both her clients and herself. It is a delight to be Martyn's coach.

Martyn and Jo Speak: We hope you've enjoyed your time with us as we've shared our coaching journey with you. It has truly been a pleasure to bring our story to you and we hope you have found it entertaining, informative, and dare we say it, inspirational. We wish you peace and happiness in your own personal journey.

About Martyn

Martyn A. Dell is the founder of Joyful Changes Coaching, a coaching practice based in London, Ontario, that specializes in coaching gay, lesbian, bisexual, transgender, and questioning people between the ages of 18 and 40. Life experiences coupled with coaching skills from The Coaching Institute have created a passion for helping members of the GLBTQ community in coming out issues and living their authentic lives. She is determined to help her clients integrate their sexuality with the rest of their lives so that they may live peaceful, joyful, and fulfilling lives. Coaching is Martyn's way of making a contribution to the world.

Prior to becoming a Certified Comprehensive Life Coach, Martyn gained 16 years of customer service experience in diverse fields such as libraries, retail stores, call centre tech support, Federal and Provincial government legal departments, and non-profit organizations.

Martyn is the co-author, with 9 other coaches, of the book **In Her Power** which helps women discover their power through chapters on purpose, peace, and play.

She is also a contributor to the second volume of Top Coaches Share which is entitled **12 Top Coaches Share Their**

Personal Power Strategies. In this collection, Martyn shared her power of faith in herself and the Universe.

Martyn believes that everyone can create limitless joy from change and that being gay, lesbian, bisexual, or transgendered does not have to prevent you from living an extraordinary life of happiness.

Contact Information:
Martyn A. Dell
martyn@joyfulchangescoaching.com
(519) 672-8013

About Jo

Josephine Romano is an acclaimed teacher, coach, facilitator, and family advocate and deeply believes in the power of leadership as parent, manager, and the innate wisdom within to create the life and work you love.

Jo is a Certified Comprehensive Life Coach and a Certified Personal Coach Trainer. She has a passion for coaching Parents, Lawyers, Managers and Women and Men in Transition to succeed and serves her clients worldwide.

She is a Nationally Certified Substance Abuse Prevention Consultant, and a Certified Teacher in Adult Dialogue Education with Global Learning Partners, Inc. She has 20 years experience in human resource management, parenting, family dynamics, child abuse, domestic violence, divorce and the courts.

A Former Court Administrator and Community Organizer, Jo has managed complex systems and human resources for over 30 years. She provides consultation to community coalitions, private and non-profit governmental agencies, and to corporations. She presents the technology to create a coaching culture within organizations that promotes high employee morale and increased profits.

She is acclaimed for her facilitation skills, which combine training design, and delivery that is meaningful, useful, and relevant to the participant.

Contact information:
Josephine Romano, CCC, CSAP
A Parent, Lawyer, and Manager's Coach
Facilitator, Consultant, and Trainer
www.greenmountainlifecoach.com
www.lifecoachforlawyers.com
www.cppcow.com

Taking Action is a Pleasurable Journey

By Eng. Yasmin Abouelhassan

Action vs. No Action

There is a great debate whether people should play it hard (take action) or use the Law of Attraction. Using the law of attraction means create positive energy, focus towards what we want to achieve in our lives, and then watch it happen. The law of attraction does not mean that we take our hands off and claim that positive energy will bring it all to us (although it is a tempting way of thinking and may be true). Indeed, focusing our energy and thoughts on what we want to feel, have or want to be, is the key to balancing our emotional level and thus creating the enthusiasm and power to take a step. When we take the smallest step, new opportunities unfold and new options open up. We move from a state of uncertainty and complete darkness to a place where we can see some light even if it is at the end of our pathway.

Everyone has the right to choose how they will lead their life as long as they are aware of their beliefs, thoughts, attitudes, actions and can take full responsibility for them.

Types of Actions

Actions are of different types:

1. **Desirable actions** are actions that we like to take. Such as doing something we like or enjoy, or doing it with someone we enjoy spending time with or because we think we'll be happy if we do it. The challenges we face with this type of actions are the time and effort for accomplishment.

2. **Should do actions** are either functioning actions or duty actions or sometimes work actions too. The challenge here is that we feel they are a burden, and something we cannot escape from. This feeling, when thought about over and over, makes us hate the action or reach an unconscious feeling of discomfort, having a heavy load, or even of imprisonment. We then develop a lot of internal resistance, and a desire to escape doing this action. If we cannot, we might build resentment towards those who push us to do those actions or those who need those actions. This is the most dangerous type of action.

3. **Dream actions** are actions that we would love to take. These are actions we wish for, yet we may or may not step into doing them. The challenge here is whether to stay in the comfort zone of dreams or jump into action steps. What keeps us in our comfort zone can be related to fear of failure, inability to take risks, inhibiting self beliefs, and sometimes the contribution of people around.

When facing a problem taking action, it is important to know which type of action it is, to allow us tailor our strategy to move forward.

Roadblocks to taking action

Although we classified types of Action and talked in brief about their challenges; there are more roadblocks that are common to all action types.

1) Internal Roadblocks

i. Questioning the value of our action
A limiting internal attitude that starts to question if the action we are about to do is of real value. Whether we are trying to do a desirable action, a duty action or a dream action, we tend to underestimate the value that this action might have on ourselves and/or on others who are affected by it. Doing so weakens our enthusiasm and starts a doubt cycle that ends in not taking any action.

ii. Lack of self Knowledge
When we don't know enough about ourselves, we let our limiting beliefs jump in. We doubt our capability of taking this action and we keep asking ourselves if we can do it or not. At times this allows the path too for old beliefs that are built-in due to old negative comments from parents, teachers, colleagues or people we met. Lack of self knowledge makes us unaware of our own motivators, passions, and triggers. When we lack self knowledge we don't know the fuel that is needed for our forward movement. Lack of self knowledge allows for self doubt and hesitation; thus contributes to lowering our energy level towards a specific action.

iii. **Fear**
Fear of the unknown; fear of failure; fear of rejection are all types of fear that limit our progress in taking actions. Fear is a natural feeling however it is only a matter of how we think. It may also be related to old beliefs, unresolved feelings, perceptions or sometimes our own protection methods... By allowing fear to take over and avoiding what initiates the fear we think we'll be in a better and safer position. However fear needs handling and effort to be tamed. It may need a talk with our coach or may need us to go through it level by level to go to the deeper real reason behind those fears in order to start handling the core of those fears. The good news is when we handle each type of fear and act in the direction of its resolution, we start building our own record of conquering fear and thus developing our skills in handling those fears or new ones when they evolve.

iv. **Negative self talk**
Negative Self-talk is the greatest inhibitor of all. This is the continuous internal voice that if left unconsciously on, leads to serious stagnation, moreover can be responsible for our setbacks. Negative self talk destructs our self confidence, attacks our self worth, and underestimates our abilities and a lot more. In dealing with negative self talk, we need primarily to recognize it. And that is by checking on the feelings accompanying those thoughts. Feelings of being drained, having low energy level, de-motivated to do anything, self pity, anger, are examples of negative feelings resulting from negative self talk. We all experience this. To conquer it, we recognize it, stop a minute and write this self talk down, then examine how it makes us feel. Does this feeling help us to move forward or keep us entangled and stuck? Does it help us enjoy our time or make us miserable and sad? Does it inspire our imagination and ideas or keep us circulating in negative and painful memories? Also, we can look around and see what the

world is sending us, if we find all what we get is negative, painful and hurting then most probable we are the ones who hurt ourselves from inside. If this is the case we can never step for an action before a decision to eliminate this negative self-talk is taken.

v. **Setting ourselves to NO-Action**
There is an illusion or a false action state and that is when we claim we are aiming to take action but the way we are doing it is unhealthy thus does not really support us in taking actions; and this is normally done by:

- **Using big indefinite words**
To really take an action, we have to always be specific as to what we want to do. If we find ourselves stuck with big words and vague tasks, we have to dig deeper, think about what this means to us, how we can attain this goal and keep digging till we can have a clear list of what exactly to do.

- **Setting Overwhelming tasks**
A lot of times we target so high. We think that by placing big tasks as goals we will push ourselves to achievements.

On the contrary it is inhibiting, because we tend to think "that's too much", "how can I accomplish this" and the thought of how big already make us feel tired.

We need to tame ourselves here a little bit; we need to make the task appeal to our capabilities, time, and effort. So we need to always break the overwhelming task into very small doable actions. Doing so, we motivate ourselves to do them and build our self confidence based on our achievements.

2) External Roadblocks
i. Choosing wrong support groups
We can be great at handling all our internal roadblocks (which take work and effort) and finally start talking about what actions we have worked ourselves to take. And suddenly we find a lot of criticism, attacks, judgments, negative comments or behaviors from those around us. Sometimes we are unconscious to the fact that not all our close relatives, family members, friends, colleagues, etc. are really supportive to us. They may have good intentions but practicing unsuitable ways with us.

ii. Interruptions
When we set ourselves for taking actions we get a lot of interruptions; we can have phone calls, people asking for advices or others who need help. We may also face close people who have other plans at the same time. The key for this roadblock is clarifying our limits and boundaries in a polite, respectful and positive way and co-creating an action plan that fit both our needs as well as theirs. This needs practice from us. If we choose not to protect our limits and boundaries, we risk not taking any action we intend to.

My Action Strategy - Inner path
The WHY

Any action we are about to take need to be verified inside us logically as well as emotionally. The more we connect to both our logic with our feelings, the closer we are to achievement. We need to clarify; why are we doing it? Who will benefit? How it will make us feel? The more we dig and become clear on the "Why" the closer we are to achievement.

In doing so the key is being completely honest with ourselves and challenging ourselves to more and more values as possible. If doing a "Should do" action we try to dig deep as to how doing it will make us feel (from the positive side); may be happy that a task is done, may be relieved that we have one task omitted from our list, maybe we will make another person happy, relieved, satisfied or thankful. Even if it is a dream action, imagine how it will make us feel, what we will gain and how our life will change if we certainly have this action done.

Tips:

- Connect with our deepest core and be honest
- Trust our deep feelings
- See the value of it to me and to others

Set the Mindset

Our mindset either creates the suitable encouraging environment that makes our action easy going or creates extra burdens on our shoulder that the action seems intolerable. To set our mindset we need to understand:

The Power of thoughts

There are two ways to handle a task /action /goal:
a) **Allowing Pattern:** "I can do it by doing:...,...",
b) **Limiting Pattern:** "I can't do it because of :.. , ... ,....."

All our achievements or un-achievements are the outputs of our thoughts, so if we keep thinking that it is too hard, overwhelming, heavy, and painful; it will be. If we think it is doable, can be fun, can add value and is challenging and exciting, it will be too. I find no words except the quote that my coach once told me:

> *If we think we can do a thing or think we can't do a thing, we're right.* Henry Ford,

I choose to think that I always can do whatever I set myself to do.

1. **The Power of Law of Attraction**
   The law of attraction states: "We attract whatever we choose to give our attention to--whether wanted or unwanted." I like this Law of Attraction theory and I love the focusing principle on the greatness, as well as holding positive energy.

   The truth is that those three together help us enjoy the moment, away from fear, anxiety, doubt and worry (which are our true enemies). When we leave our doubts to jump and our faith to slip away we are attacked severely by those 4 monsters. They spoil our time, steal our sleep, make our heart ache and above all make us wait for the worst to happen. Through this mixture of negative feelings, our energy drains away and we are left there helpless, motivation-less and life-less.

   Tips:
   - Choose to use the mixture of Law of Attraction.
   - Focus on greatness.
   - Maintain positive energy.
   - Have faith.

2. **The Power of Intention**
   Setting the Intention is adjusting our focus and collecting our thoughts, feelings and programming our brain to the state of doing. With setting the intention, we may say our prayers too and make sure our intentions are for a real value thus adding to our faith of being able to take the action.

3. **The Power of Passion**
   Our passion is the fuel for our action, it is a built in passion if we are going to take a desirable action, however if it is a should do action; we may need to create a passion about it to help us do it (Discover what steps we like most and how we can benefit or add a value to ourselves while doing it- or we may even discover our passion in servicing/ helping others). Finally for our dream actions, we certainly will have passion around dreaming about it, we'll twist it a little to develop a passion of doing it by connecting to our inner feelings as to why thinking about it makes us happy. A key for all action types is to sustain our passion level that will help us take this action. Our passion maintains our positive energy.

4. **The Power of Enjoyment**
   Remember we are not here to be tortured throughout our life; we are here to enjoy every journey we take. Journeys can be of self discovery, of learning, of acquiring skills, of meeting challenges as well as deadlines. Finding the fun part in actions we want to do is a key to enjoying the journey. Actions need to be

done any how so why waste a chance of enjoyment. We deserve the fun.

5. **The Power of Faith**
   Faith is a key component to the mixture, and it actually what makes us eliminate the doubts (that jump in our minds) challenging the action. The thought of "if this is what it takes then why are all those people suffering." Actually people are suffering because they don't know about the law of attraction and how it works. And even knowing is not all what it takes, because if we are half hearted about it (still have doubts) our energy level will not be positive and thus we will not achieve what we aim for and the cycle of doubt comes to be a belief. Faith plays this role and it is different, if we have high self confidence we can have faith in ourselves and in our capabilities, power, talents and achievement. But if our self confidence swings or our dreams are real challenging then we need faith of higher powers. For me I have faith in God to bring me what I set my energy and focus at and this makes my doubts settle and makes me really attract what I want. Faith will keep us on track. Make us stretch our schedule a little, our abilities a little, and voila things will be done. Keeping the faith makes the job easier.

6. **The Power of Visualization**
   Visualization is a mental activity of seeing our action done and seeing the celebration we deserve. It maintains our direction, keeps our energy levels high and makes the journey worth traveling. It also helps our mind to assist us in achieving our goals. It dissipates the

doubts because we visualize our dreams coming true. This takes us from one action to the next and keeps the momentum.

I visualize what I set my energy and focus for. Because even with the faith; we sometimes divert to "what ifs" or may lose focus. But with some extra mind exercise of visualizing the success or the achievement moment .WOW... my energy level boosts, and the greatest is that my imagination starts thinking about what actions may I take to help manifesting what I want. Here it does not come from a place of should do but from a place of fun, enjoyment and pleasure and I feel it just flows inside me with a flood of ideas and scenarios.

Ordinary people believe only in the possible. Extraordinary people visualize not what is possible or probable, but rather what is impossible. And by visualizing the impossible, they begin to see it as possible. Cherie Carter-Scott

Outer Path

The outer part is the mini action stage where we take tiny organizing actions.

i. **Jot down our thoughts**
   (Be honest) when we are about to take an action, writing down our thoughts instead of making them float into our mind. Doing so, frees a lot of space on our mind thus eliminating a lot of tension too that is encountered by thinking about taking an action. When we have our thoughts in front of us, we can examine them as to which is positive so serving us and which is not thus hindering us. Then we can choose consciously what thoughts to focus at and what needs verification. We can ask for our coach's help with that or do it by ourselves or with a trusted friend.

ii. **Make a list of required actions**
As writing helped us with our thoughts, it will again with our list of required actions. If I leave my list of action to just pass through my mind then I am risking that they will only be day dreams, but being aware of that I just grab the first pen and piece of paper I can reach and start throwing out my ideas or my action list. Not giving it much thought, I just make them flow, because the more I write the more I create space for more to flow and more to come.
At this level, I am ready to do next extra mental effort. Sort them according to our preference either urgency or dependency on each other or time needed. Don't forget to assign the estimated realistic time for each too, this will help us decide as to what needs to be done first.

iii. **Break it into baby steps**
Take the first action we listed and break it into baby steps, the smallest possible steps. Just throw them on a piece of paper randomly as they pop in our mind. In front of each step assign a treat we're going to do to ourselves when accomplishing each step. Use simple do-able treats that we can enjoy. (Fresh Juice, 10 min. of watching T.V. undisturbed, a warm shower, a small cup of coffee, whatever small thing that we don't get time to enjoy through our day and that will not be accompanied by self blame (extra calories – unhealthy food - ..Etc)

Top Coaches Share Their Personal Action Strategies

> iv. **The Now step (the smallest task to take)**
> Have a thorough look over our listed baby steps and decide on only one to be done now.
>
> v. **Do it NOW**
> Don't procrastinate, jump and do it now.
>
> vi. **Create our baby success Journal**
> When we see it done; write it down on our baby success journal. Make it colorful, reachable (near our desk or on the refrigerator or beside our mirror); in a place that we can see every day. And any further step we accomplish go and write it there too with a big red sign of achievement, a joyful sticker whatever makes us happy and feel our achievement.
>
> vii. **Celebrate baby achievements**
> Now take the time and celebrate our achievement.
>
> viii. **Share our celebrations with our support Group**
> We can further celebrate by sharing our achievement with one or our entire support group family members, friends, our coach or whoever we choose. Only make sure those are people who will celebrate our success and share the fun.

Doing so makes my day, puts a smile on my face, a relief at my heart and helps me enjoy my moment and take the action.

Top Coaches Share Their Personal Action Strategies

You can do it on your own. Just Try. If you are stuck with taking action, or can't enjoy the journey enough... Hire a Coach.

About Yasmin

Eng. Yasmin Abouelhassan, Certified Comprehensive Coach, President and Founder Happy Family Institute

www.happyfamilyinstitute.org
www.hfi4u.com

Yasmin was a Biomedical Engineer with 12 years experience in sales and management of medical supplies and equipment.

Using her expertise in building and maintaining customer relations as well as her extensive qualifications in sales, and her strong *management* background with a proven ability to create and boost a healthy team spirit within work team has definitely added to her success in coaching both people and organizations within her 3 years specific experience as a Certified Comprehensive Coach; coaching individuals and organizations towards their specific goals and challenges.

Now the founder and president of Happy Family Institute which is the first coaching service provider in Egypt.

Through individual life coaching; She coach her clients around communication skills, building and maintaining healthy relationships, understanding and excelling in their personal and professional lives. Through coaching she helps company's management address different paths for the achievement of their missions and goals, current situation analysis, job analysis, personnel planning and recruiting, personnel follow-up and coaching, conducting or advising requested trainings.

Through coaching, she personally conducts training courses for sales, management, and customer service

Yasmin says "For me one of the keys to ultimate happiness is when my clients (whom I really love and sincerely care for) step to successes in their personal and professional lives, when confidence takes its path in their soul, when they commit themselves to taking actions, develop and start their happy journey, I feel deep inside that this is why I existed on earth this is why GOD has created me and this is my destiny to live for."

Contact Information:
Eng. Yasmin Abouelhassan
www.happyfamilyinstitute.org
www.hfi4u.com
(202) 27002715
(202) 27010415

Additional Information

If you are interested in reading more Top Coaches Share Books or finding information about your favorite Coach visit the Top Coaches Share Website at www.topcoachesshare.com

Printed in the United States
108102LV00003B/37-93/P